CHRIST, JUSTICE AND PEACE

CHRIST, JUSTICE AND PEACE
Toward a Theology of the State
in Dialogue with the Barmen Declaration

EBERHARD JÜNGEL

Translated by
D. Bruce Hamill and
Alan J. Torrance

With an Introductory Essay by
Alan J. Torrance

T&T CLARK
EDINBURGH

T&T CLARK
59 GEORGE STREET
EDINBURGH EH2 2LQ
SCOTLAND

Authorised English Translation of *Barmen;*
Kirche Zwischen Versuchung und Gnade
by Ernst Wolf, published by Chr. Kaiser Verlag, 1984

First published 1992

ISBN 0 567 29212 6

British Library Cataloguing-in-Publication Data
A catalogue record for this book
is available from the British Library

Typeset by Trinity Typesetting, Edinburgh
Printed and bound in Great Britain by
Martins of Berwick

Contents

Translators' Preface

There was a rumour in Tübingen that when one of Professor Jüngel's earlier books was pronounced untranslatable by an English publisher he held a party to celebrate! The two of us are proud to form part of a growing conspiracy of people determined that he be deprived of such opportunities for celebration. Having said this, however, we are inclined to think that completing the translation of a work by Professor Jüngel, no matter how short, does warrant such festivities on the part of the translators! Professor Jüngel's lengthy sentences, subtle nuances and word-plays do not make the translator's task an easy one. This is not in any way to seek to decry his writing but rather to make the point that communicating fully the genius of his theological insight and expression in English is not as straightforward as one might hope.

For this reason, we undertook the safeguard of having a native German speaker, who is also a theologian, produce an initial translation into English to serve as a basis and guide for our own translation of the text. Consequently, we should like to acknowledge our indebtedness to Ms. Johanna Friedlein who fulfilled this task for us and to express our warm appreciation of all her hard work.

One example of the way in which Professor Jüngel uses German is reflected in the original title, *Mit Frieden Staat zu Machen*, which involves a clever wordplay expressing the fact that the book concerns the topics of peace and the state while simultaneously communicating the fact that it is concerned to celebrate peace. We were unable to find any way of reflecting the subtlety of this in English.

A further preparatory comment we should add concerns the use of gender specific language. We have sought as far as is possible, without distorting the original text, to translate the German into 'inclusive' English.

Finally, further gratitude must be expressed to Rev. Graeme Sellers who spent considerable time reading and commenting most usefully on our English text.

D. Bruce Hamill
Alan J. Torrance

Introductory Essay
by Alan J. Torrance

It is often said that there is no such privileged option open to us as political neutrality. This argument has been used to encourage people to be politically engaged and responsible. Likewise - though it may be less fashionable to say so - there is no such privileged position as *theological* neutrality. Too often political theology, even when advocated in the name of the church, has been theologically superficial. Though it may reflect admirable sentiments and concerns, it can lack theological consistency and coherence and thus theological warrant. What Jüngel seeks to offer and to inspire in this book is interaction with those theological issues which underlie "the political existence of the Christian".

If the Church and the Gospel are not simply to be used to claim divine sanction for various world-views then much more is required than appeals to individual life experience, political ideologies and 'intuitive' ethical convictions. What is necessary here is serious theological consideration as to how precisely we do determine God's will and God's Word to us in our various contexts.

Furthermore, at a time when the church and society are becoming increasingly characterised by cultural and ethical pluralism, theological affirmation requires clarity as to the theological criteria which operate in relation to our God-talk within the Christian faith. This requires us to ask questions of the form: What is the nature of the critical controls upon our attempts to interpret the divine intention? What are the theological grounds of the socio-political claims we make? How far does the specific and concrete Word of God to humankind in Christ require a revision of our intuitive interpretations of the nature and function of the state and of its obligations and responsibilities for justice, peace and freedom? How far does the Word, as the impetus and warrant for God-talk within the political domain, involve a semantic reconstruction of these terms reorienting their meaning rather than simply endorsing their everyday usage? These questions are of fundamental importance if there is to be responsible and integrative engagement with socio-political issues and if we are to avoid further fragmentation and division within the church and society with different parties indulging in claims of divine sanction for their various perspectives.

The social context from which the Barmen declaration emerged in Germany in 1934, was one where prior cultural and nationalistic (one could say 'indigenous') agendas were prescribing and determining the church's political perspectives together with its theological affirmations and, indeed, self-affirmations. Within the church theological programs were conditioned by a primary concern with Germany's own indigenous identity and with establishing the rich culture of its people. This arose in part as an understandable consequence of the humiliation of Germany which followed the First World War and a resulting desire to recover a sense of nationhood and self-respect. The result, however, was that the specific imperatives of the Gospel were too easily confined to a spiritualised sphere of subjective piety - what the Neo-Kantians (and the 'culture Protestants' whose thinking they shaped) termed the sphere of the *Individuum*, the home of faith and religion. What is striking, however, is how prominent and widespread certain features of this approach are in our contemporary theological scene. A concern with national, cultural and ethnic self-identity which relegates the concrete and specific assertions of the Gospel to a spiritualised realm, can be seen to characterise much contemporary "ecclesial" theology worldwide.

The theologians who met at Barmen stood against the stream of 'culture Protestantism' and civil religion by making two central affirmations. First, there is no area of human life over which Christ is not Lord. This means that the one Word whom we are to trust and obey in life and death can neither be localised within some prior, subjective realm of individual piety nor translated into some form of cultural self-affirmation. Second, to confess the Lordship of Christ over all areas of life (intellectual and cultural, ecclesial and civil) means that, in the light of the Gospel, we are unconditionally obliged to be true and obedient to the One who is in his person God's Word to humankind. Culture, therefore, may neither determine the sphere of the Gospel nor relativise its imperatives but, conversely, culture and society require to be perceived, interpreted and evaluated critically in the light of the Gospel.

This is reflected powerfully in Dietrich Bonhoeffer's lectures on Christology where he emphasises that we must never interpret the Logos or the Word as the divine endorsement of any prior, human programs (*logoi*) or as the ratification of prior, human 'speech' to or from our society, religion or culture. There is no respect in which any prior world-view or cultural self-understanding can serve to accommodate, within what would always be a Procrustean bed, the One who is God's once and for all Word to humankind.

Rather, to the extent that Christ is the Logos of God he stands as the Counter-logos to our preconceived social, cultural, political and religious conceptualities. As such he radically revises and reorders the prior blueprints with which we intuitively desire to shape our world and interpret our experience. Therefore, far from perfecting prior social, cultural and political ends, the Gospel of grace, as it becomes event in the person of the Logos, stands to redefine all our social, cultural and political values and loyalties.

The relevance to the contemporary debate of this challenge is reflected in the enormous interest in recent years on the part of South African theologians in the Barmen declaration and those associated with it. However, it should be clear to the reader that the relevance of these questions extends well beyond South Africa, indeed, to the contemporary church worldwide.

In this book, Jüngel is concerned primarily with the relevance of the fifth thesis of Barmen for church-state relations and the preservation of peace, justice and freedom. However, he discusses it within the theological framework of the Declaration as a whole, articulating with theological depth its inner logic and seeking to explore its significance for our engagement with the question of peace and church-state relations today.

Attention here should be drawn to several important features which reflect the thrust and direction of Jüngel's argumentation.

First, his approach is characterised by his professed concern for a theology that has ecclesial character and manifests "reverence of thought". There is therefore no enthusiasm on his part for engaging in "hasty decrees".

Second, his discussion emphasises the affirmative nature of the Gospel stressing the fact that negations have no meaning or function independently of God's 'Yes'. Where the church can find it easier, and believe it to be more relevant, to engage in negations - negative exhortations and condemnations - Jüngel stresses the extent to which Barmen had something far more important to say than any mere 'No'. Rather, its primary concern was to affirm the 'Yes' which has already been spoken by God in Jesus Christ. The heart of the Gospel is therefore the 'inconceivable' and unconditional divine *affirmation* of humanity, its inalienable value before God and God's identification with it.

"The meaning of the Barmen Declaration for the church's task today... consists in learning anew what is meant by, 'Lo! I am with you always till the end of the world.'... Listening to this 'I' means stating positively what is to be affirmed validly as evangelical truth in the context of a world which is increasingly setting in motion its own apocalyptic devastation."

Third, he is concerned to make categorically clear that, if we are to exclude the worship of Christ-images, ideologies of Christ, Jesus-cults and suchlike, there must be no separation of *solus Christus* from *sola Scriptura.* Jüngel shows how easy it was for the German Christians, by detaching Christ from Scripture, to redefine Christ as the exemplification of the truly heroic way of life and where the cross, like the Swastika, became simply a symbol for the ideal of sacrifice.

Fourth, Jüngel appeals for a move beyond traditional forms of natural theology to what he terms a '*more natural* theology'. Much political theology has been grounded in an appeal to a natural theology whereby God's purposes for humanity are read 'out of' nature by the light of 'natural' reason. If this kind of approach has led to affirmative theories of natural rights and the discernment of human equality in certain contexts it has also led to precisely the opposite conclusions in others. It has failed to challenge the oppression of 'inferior races' or a 'weaker sex' by claims to 'natural discernment' and descriptions of God's intentions read out of an alleged 'natural order'.

Jüngel offers a profoundly new alternative to the forms of natural theology which failed so tragically in Nazi Germany and South Africa - and which continue to fail women by way of the naturalistic categories undergirding canon law in various sectors of the church. He suggests a '*more natural* theology' which recognises Jesus Christ as the one who has reconciled both human beings and also the world. Here the range and scope of soteriology is rethought in such a manner that 'new ways open up': ways which open up for women and men new forms of engagement with political and ecological issues. These are new ways which, he suggests, lead out *from* God's Word in Christ to the world as 'ways to nature and to history - ways of knowledge and life which lead ever more deeply into this world as God's creation.' These ways, take us not only into the joys of the created order but into compassionate solidarity with those who cry out for God from their very depths or further, he suggests, with those 'who may not even be able to cry at all in their misery'. In other words, he advocates a form of theology which is far more effectively orientated towards nature than traditional forms of 'natural theology' and which takes much more seriously the challenge of the alienation of the created order and the widespread human suffering associated with this.

My final reference is to Jüngel's radical critique of the contemporary tendency to reduce Christianity to moralism and the Gospel to an '*epistle of morality* - with all its demands and unattainable obligations'. This kind of approach leads to the degeneration of the church into a moral institution throwing people back upon themselves and on to resources which they are neither able to produce nor, in the face of such exhortations, would ever have the energy or the will to call upon. This is the very opposite of liberation and it is the inversion of the Gospel! As Jüngel points out, 'It is only, indeed, as our whole life is *liberated* that it ever becomes a *whole* life, a *healed* life'. It is this that 'distinguishes Jesus Christ - as he claims our whole life - from all totalitarian demands, among which the moralistic demand is probably the basic model of a totalitarian claim on human life. None of these totalitarian demands liberate life. Rather they *violate* it because they lay claim to our whole life *without* being able to *make it whole.*' Totalitarian demands can only lead the sinner deeper into the disintegration of his or her own existence.

The righteousness that characterises the will of God is not a righteousness that condemns.

Rather, it is a 'righteousness that justifies the sinner'. This requires us to rethink the very form of any theological critique of social sin. The impetus for repentance and the transformation of our thinking (*metanoia*) at this level is this same righteousness which justifies the sinner, the righteousness of the one who accepts, transforms and liberates the sinner in an act of unconditional love, as is reflected in the story of Zacchaeus. The Gospel gives rise to evangelical social repentance (repentance as a response to the indicatives of grace) rather then legal social repentance (repentance as a human endeavour grounded merely on some ethical or legal mandate).

It is, moreover, precisely here that we discover what Jüngel terms "the inviolable value of the human person". In other words, the Church is obliged to look nowhere else than to this Word of grace for the provision of the categories which it must strive to establish both in public policy and at the constitutional level.

In sum, it is the indicatives of grace which carry the imperatives of obligation - 'the pledge of liberation through Jesus Christ carries his claim on our whole life'. It is the healing of humanity in and through God's reconciling Word to humanity which is the ground and impetus of our socio-political interpretation and commitment. Consequently, it is in what

Barmen and Jüngel point to here that we find the theological form that a theology of the state must take - one that is both positive and constructive and yet also critical, but always in that order.

In conclusion, I have sought to draw attention to some of the central theological affirmations from which Jüngel seeks to commence the task of working out a theology of the state. What is immediately clear is that these commit one to a theologically much more radical approach than those forms of approach which make recourse to 'foreign' categories and notions affirmed independently and in advance of God's Word to humankind. What is important to notice is the extent to which this approach obviates the need to appeal to such inherently risk-laden notions as the following: "orders of creation"; naturalistic anthropological categories; individualistic theories of God-given rights; divinely ordained legal decrees and categories; cultural mandates; indigenous self-understandings. Categories such as these can lead all too easily to predicating divine sovereignty of the capacity of 'natural reason' and its dictates!

The articulation of a theological understanding of the state and its responsibility for the preservation of justice and peace is clearly the task of all Christians to the extent that they *are not* and *cannot be* 'neutral' in either the theological or the socio-political spheres. Jüngel's engagement with these issues in continuity and dialogue with Barmen exemplifies the theological seriousness with which we are to wrestle with the questions of our "political existence".

One's hope is that this process may encourage us to move beyond "political theologies" to "theological politics" - a theologically driven approach to the state rather than a politically driven approach to God. This would involve an approach which interprets our responsibilities *to* the state and *within* the state in the light of God's inclusive, recreative and healing purposes held forth in God's Word of grace to humanity. Such an approach to society, to culture, to the state and to the ecosystem would be both more *radical* and more *liberating* - theologically and politically - than so much that has sought in recent times to lay claim to these attributes.

Knox Theological Hall,
Dunedin,
New Zealand.

THE BARMEN THEOLOGICAL DECLARATION
A New Translation

DOUGLAS S. BAX

(From: Journal of Theology for Southern
Africa, June 1984 No. 47)

*The Barmen Theological Declaration was first pub-
lished in 1934. The English translation of it com-
monly used since 1962*[1] *has been that offered by
Arthur C. Cochrane in his important pioneering work
in the English language,* The Church's Confession under Hitler, *which was published that year.*[2]
*Ever since I first studied the Declaration as a gradu-
ate student in the 1960s, however, I have been dis-
satisfied with this translation. Cochrane himself noted
that the Declaration was difficult to translate, and
that his translation was in places 'awkward'.*[3] *After
much wrestling with the German text I have become*

---

[2] Philadelphia: Westminster, p. 239-242.
[3] *Op. cit.*, p. 239 n. 2.

*convinced that a translation which conveys its mean-
ing both more precisely and more idiomatically is
possible.*[4] *I therefore attempt in what follows to provide such a translation.*

*The original German text of the Declaration is
available in several works. I have followed it in
Gerhard Niemoller's* Die erste Bekenntnissynode
der Deutschen Evangelischen Kirche zu Barmen, *Vol. II* Text — Dokumente — Berichte.[5]

In view of the errors of the 'German Christians' and[6] of the present Reich Church Administration, which are ravaging the Church
and at the same time also shattering the unity
of the German Evangelical Church, we confess the following evangelical truths:

1. 'I am the Way and the Truth and the Life;
   no one comes to the Father except through
   me.' (Jn. 14:6)
   Truly, truly I say to you, he who does not
   enter the sheepfold through the door but
   climbs in somewhere else, he is a thief and

[4] I also wish to thank Gottfried Krautz for discussing
a few of the more abstruse points of translation with me.

[5] Gottingen: Vandenhoeck & Ruprecht, 1959, p. 198-
202.

[6] Cochrane (or his printers?) here made an important mistranslation by omitting the 'and'. The Declaration was addressed in the first place to the Church and
the 'German Christians' in it and only in the second
place to the State and the Church Administration im-
posed on the Church.

a robber. I am the Door; if anyone enters through me, he will be saved.' (Jn. 10:1, 9)[7]

Jesus Christ, as he is attested to us in Holy Scripture, is the one Word of God which we have to hear, and which we have to trust and obey in life and in death.

We reject the false doctrine that the Church could and should recognise[8] as a source of its proclamation, beyond and besides this one Word of God, yet other events, powers, historic figures,[9] and truths[10] as God's revelation.[11]

---

[7] Cochrane used the RSV for the quotations from the Bible. With the greater variety of modern translation now available, I have found it difficult to choose any one version. I have therefore made my own translation of the biblical texts, seeking to bring out relevant nuances.

[8] For *als könne und müsse die Kirche anerkennen* Cochrane rejects the translation 'that the Church can and must acknowledge'; he prefer the more literal 'as though the Church could and would have to acknowledge'. This, he explains, is in order to express 'a characteristic point in Barth's theology and in the Barmen Declaration, namely, that sin and evil do not have a positive existence as that which is created and willed by God' (p. 239 n. 2). This translation, however, sacrifices both grammar and intelligibility. I have tried to express the same point more intelligibly and with better grammar by using 'that' but retaining the subjunctive. In the negative clauses of the second, third and fourth theses I have also resorted to adding a subjunctive 'could'.

[9] *Gestalten* in the sense of formative figures on the stage of history. ('German Christians' spoke of Hitler as

2. 'Jesus Christ has been made wisdom and righteousness and sanctification and redemption for us by God.' (1 Cor. 1:30).

As Jesus Christ is God's comforting pronouncement of the forgiveness of all our sins, so, and with equal seriousness, he is also God's vigorous announcement of his claim upon our whole life.[12] Through him

the German Moses.) To make the meaning clear in English I have added the adjective 'historic'. See further Cochrane, A.C.: op. cit., p. 239 n. 2.

[10] Ernst Wolf instances what is being referred to by these four German words as follows:

* events: Hitler's takeover of power in the Spring of 1933
* powers: *Blut und Boden* ('blood and soil')
* figures: Adolf Hitler himself
* truths: ideology concerning the *Volk*

(Wolf, E.: *Barmen. Kirche zwischen Versuchung und Gnade* (Munchen: Chr. Kaiser, 1957), p. 104.)

[11] The punctuation of this sentence is a problem. The phrase 'as a source of its proclamation' was a late addition to the original draft (Niemoller, G.: *op. cit.*, Vol. I, *Geschichte, Kritik und Bedeutung der Synode und ihre Theologischen Erklarung*, p. 99). The addition renders the whole sentence clumsy. It can therefore be argued that this phrase rather than the next should be marked off with commas. This, however, would make the sentence more difficult to follow without really adding precision. (The effect of this added phrase is that though it seems to allow more room in a formal sense for the idea of general or natural revelation, it really excludes it in any material sense, i.e. as an alternative or supplementary source of the Church's message besides Scripture.)

there comes to us joyful liberation from the godless ties of this world[13] **for free, grateful service to his creatures.**

We reject the false doctrine that there could be areas of our life in which we would belong not to Jesus Christ but to other lords, areas in which we would not need justification and sanctification through him.

3. 'Let us, however, speak the truth in love, and in every respect grow into him who is the head, into Christ, from whom the whole body is joined together.' (Eph. 4:15-16)

   The Christian Church is the community of brethren in which, in Word and sacrament, through the Holy Spirit, Jesus Christ

---

[12] The force of this sentence partly depends on the play on the German words *Zuspruch* and *Anspruch*. Cochrane felt this play could not be expressed in English (p. 240 n.3). However, if one translates *Zuspruch* 'comforting pronouncement' and *kraftiger Anspruch* 'vigorous announcement of His claim', this expresses both the play on words and the attention their common root draws to the nature of this claim as God's Word. 'Comforting pronouncement' is in any case more precise (and more suitable here) as a translation of *Zuspruch* than Cochrane's 'assurance'. The point being made is not precisely that Christ assures us of forgiveness but that, having himself been made our 'righteousness', he is the one in and through whom our forgiveness is effectively declared in the first place.

[13] What is meant here is particularly the ideologically perverted ties of *Volk* and race.

acts in the present as Lord.[14] With both its faith and its obedience, with both its message and its order, it has to testify in the midst of the sinful world, as the Church of pardoned sinners, that it belongs to him alone and lives and may[15] live by his comfort and under his direction alone, in expectation of his appearing.[16]

We reject the false doctrine that the Church could have permission to hand over the form of its message and of its order to whatever it itself might wish or to the vicissitudes of the prevailing ideological and political convictions of the day.

4. 'You know that the rules of the Gentiles exercise authority over them and those in high position lord it over them. So shall it not be among you; but if anyone would have authority among you, let him be your servant.'

[14] Part of the point involved here (and a subject of discussion in the drafting committee) is that Christ is present in the sacrament, as both Luther and Calvin taught. To bring out this point *gegenwärtig handelt* could perhaps be translated 'is present and acts'.

[15] Cochrane incorrectly translates *mochte* as 'wants' instead of in its auxiliary sense.

[16] 'Appearing' rather than 'appearance' (Cochrane), because the reference is to in (II Thess. 2:8), I Tim. 6:14, II Tim 1:10, 4:1, 8, Tit. 2:13, where it is usually translated 'appearing'.

(Matt. 20:25-26)

The various offices in the Church do not provide a basis for some to exercise authority over others but for the ministry with which the whole community has been entrusted and charged to be carried out.

We reject the false doctrine that, apart from this ministry, the Church could, and could have permission to, give itself or allow itself to be given special leaders (*Fuhrer*)[17] vested with ruling authority.

5. 'Fear God, honour the King!' (I Pet. 2:17)

Scripture tells us that by divine appointment[18] the State, in this still unredeemed world in which also the Church is situated, has the task of maintaining justice and peace, so far as human discernment and human ability make this possible, by means of the threat and use of force. The Church acknowledges with gratitude and reverence toward God the benefit of this, his appointment. It draws attention to God's Kingdom

---

[17] In the original draft this word was placed within inverted commas, but the commas were deleted in the final draft (Niemoller, G.: *op. cit.*, Vol. II, p. 200 n. 20).

[18] *Anordnung* (to be understood in the sense of the Latin *ordinatio*) as distinct from *Ordnung* (Lt. *ordo*, Eng. 'order'), a critically important word in the orthodox German Lutheran theology of Church and State.

(Reich), **God's commandment and justice, and with these the responsibility of those who rule and those who are ruled. It trusts and obeys the power of the Word, by which God upholds all things.**

We reject the false doctrine that beyond its special commission the State should and could become the sole and total order of human life and so fulfil the vocation of the Church as well.

We reject the false doctrine that beyond its special commission the Church should and could take on the nature, tasks and dignity which belong to the State and thus become itself an organ of the State.

6. 'See, I am with you always, to the end of the age.' (Matt. 28:20)

'God's Word is not fettered.' (II Tim. 2:9)

The Church's commission, which is the foundation of its freedom, consists in this: in Christ's stead, and so in the service of his own Word and work, to deliver to all people, through preaching and sacrament, the message of the free grace of God.

We reject the false doctrine that with human vainglory the Church could place the Word and work of the Lord in the service of self-chosen desires, purposes and plans.

The Confessional Synod of the German

Evangelical Church declares that it sees in the acknowledgement of these truths and in the rejection of these errors the indispensable theological basis of the German Evangelical Church as a confederation of Confessional Churches. It calls upon all who can stand in solidarity with its Declaration to be mindful of these theological findings in all their decisions concerning Church and State. It appeals to all concerned to return to unity in faith, hope and love.

Verbum Dei manet in aeternum.

Dedication: For my sisters, Hannelore and Margarete, of whom I am proud.

Introduction

In its fifth thesis the Barmen Theological Declaration defined the responsibility of the state as being to preserve justice and peace. This is its divinely intended and 'appointed' task. The state's responsibility, defined in this manner, presents itself in different ways in accordance with different historical situations and requires, therefore, to be realised in quite different ways. This results in the fact that the church is required to think anew - and, when necessary, to reconsider - its own attitudes and responsibilities in its particular historical situation vis-a-vis the tasks of the state. The fiftieth anniversary of the (unanimously ratified) confession of Barmen has provided me with the welcome opportunity of asking - by way of a reflection on the contemporary significance of the Declaration's fifth thesis - what the church demands of the state when proclaiming her message in the present situation, and together with the Barmen fathers, that the state has, by divine appointment, the responsibility of providing for peace. This opportunity was officially occasioned by lectures given to the Synod of the

1

Evangelischen Kirche des Rheinlandes and at the Barmen anniversary-celebration of the *Evangelischen Kirche in Deutschland* and also by a course of seminars held together with my colleague Klaus Scholder in the University of Tübingen. The thoughts reflected in this *Kaiser Treatise* represent the topical counterpart to the publication in the same series which emerged in 1983, *Zum Wesen des Friedens. Frieden als Kategorie theologischer Anthropologie* , and which was oriented more specifically toward foundational principles. Unlike many publications available nowadays concerning this pressing issue of peace, I have sought - despite all the intellectual and emotional passion which is not only inevitable but also highly appropriate - to argue with utmost caution and consideration. The key thesis has been formulated, therefore, in the form of a question. Occasionally, a question expresses a perception in a more pressing way than a thesis, which I usually find more congenial. In any case, in the present discussion of peace, questions seem to me to manifest "the reverence of thought" more adequately than hasty decrees. But to avoid misunderstanding, I have to warn expressly against softening the challenge posed by my opting for the question-form. These are burning questions which call for decision.

The structure of the Treatise reflects the fact that, in my judgement, the fifth thesis of

Barmen demands to be interpreted within the context of the whole Theological Declaration. To detach it from this context would be to create the determining precondition of its misinterpretation.[1] I have first brought into focus, therefore, the systematic structure which is identical in all six theses and which is essential for their understanding. It was then necessary that the fundamental significance of the first and second theses for the whole declaration be explained. Following this there is a discussion of the fifth thesis, and this involves two steps. First, there is provided a more exegetical explanation of the text. Then, by way of a more systematic interpretation, I shall inquire into the relationship between church and state, or rather into the nature of the political existence of the Christian. The interpretation aims at a proper understanding of the state's given responsibility to provide for *peace*. The state's duty to provide for *justice*, though no less important, remains for the present in the background. The express nature and purpose of

---

[1] W. Hüber makes a similar judgement concerning the results of christian freedom. 'Ethik und theorie der Kirche im Horizont der Barmer Theologischen Erklärung '[The Ethics and Theory of the Church within the Perspective of the Barmen Theological Declaration], *NBST 4*, 1983, 96.

the Barmen Declaration would be lost if the fifth thesis were detached from its connection with the theses on the church. It lies with those who read the following explorations to establish the connection for themselves. The interested reader will find my deliberations on the confessional character of the Theological Declaration in my introduction to a collection arranged by M. Rohkrämer: *K. Barth, Texte zur Barmer Theologische Erklärung*, 1984, IX-XXII.

I have been inspired and enlightened by the aforementioned seminar with Klaus Scholder, through the common work of an EKU committee and, above all, by the critical checking of the manuscript by my assistant, Dr. Johannes Fischer, who made suggestions for more precise formulations which I was more than happy to incorporate. Let me here make special reference to his slightly different perception of the matter which he has expressed under the title, "Nein ohne jedes Ja? - Kritische Anfragen an die Erklärung des Moderamens des Reformierten Bundes zur Friedensverantwortung der Kirche" in *ZThK* 3/83, 352-372.

CHAPTER 1

I

1. The Barmen Theological Declaration has significance for the present day at least in so far as it is a classical example of how very much the Christian church depends on solid theology and of how little value there is in a theology which evades its concrete responsibility to the church. Indeed, Karl Barth made clear in 1934 that the real importance of the Barmen Synod was that the "resistance to the system which had at that time arisen"[2] had now finally taken *theological* form. Until that time, "it had often been" as if one "either worked with a theology which was no theology, or assumed that one was managing without any theology at all, and was thus unable to speak and to act out of the knowledge of faith."[3] "It is no coincidence that theology had taught over many decades that it is not so much theology that matters (and that means precisely the knowl-

---

[2] K. Barth in :*Texte zur Barmer Theologischen Erklärung,* [Texts of the Barmen Theological Declaration] published by M. Rohkrämer 1984, 25.
[3] Loc. cit., 33.

edge of faith), but rather it is life and love upon which everything hangs."[4] "The theological declaration of the synod of Barmen...has in principle brought an end to this state of affairs. The declaration means that the resistance against the regime of the German Lutheran Church now knows itself to be grounded in a recognition deriving from faith. It expresses this *recognition* and for that reason it is a *theological* declaration."[5] If this theological declaration is to have not merely general but rather specific significance, then it must serve to impress on us the necessity of theological perception, and that means solid theological work in the sphere of the church. What is asked for is not what pleases or displeases the world, neither ecclesiastical self-satisfaction nor an attitude of ecclesiastical self-accusation. Rather, what is sought is that which is recognised and confessed as "evangelical truth". This is what the church is given to pursue. It is to know the truth, however, that is the genuine task of theology. Without it the church would lose its character, it would degenerate into a characterless club for the cultivation of religion or into a no less characterless institution of clerical and administrative self-preoccupa-

[4] Loc. cit., 32.
[5] Loc. cit., 34.

tion. It is specifically within the spiritual life of
the church that the rigour of theological perception belongs.

The same should also be said, however, from
the opposite direction. The extensive failure
of a spineless university theology which shirked
its serious responsibility to the church led, in
the third Reich, to the establishment of the
seminaries of the Confessing Church. Since
then academic theology has recognised it to
be a matter of principal that it carries out its
duties vis-a-vis the university only when called
for. For that reason alone the churches in West
Germany and East Germany will do well to
maintain and to hold in honour the church
seminaries as advanced schools of academic
theology. In doing such they continue to function as a vital, institutional reminder to 'university theology'. Irrespective of what one
hopes will be a good relationship with the fac-
ulties of theology, church seminaries in this
way bind themselves to take the utmost care in
cultivating an active, academic theology within
their own areas and by their own means as
this serves to maintain the church's self-criti-
cism.

On its side, evangelical theology will con-
tinuously have to ask itself anew whether it is
worthy of its good name. For evangelical theology only exists in scholarly service to the one

Word which we are to hear and which we are to trust and obey in life and in death. Evangelical theology only exists in scholarly service to the Word which the church has to proclaim and against which, therefore, the church itself has to be measured critically. To that end theology definitely needs to take a deep breath. And what is more, it requires, beyond any doubt, academic breadth and, surely, something like academic refinement as well. Theology is not to be ashamed of being academic work at a desk and lectures given from a lectern. But academic breadth and refinement are only meaningful and justified if they spring from a *concentration*, a *collectedness* towards the one thing that is needful. Both the academic work at a desk and the lecture given from the lectern have an existential relationship to the pulpit. This does not have to be constantly and explicitly proclaimed. Academic restraint can be much more effective in this context. But it must be there - otherwise evangelical theology, in its academic form, would not only reflect a grotesque self-misunderstanding but would also dig its own grave. So much vain, academic effort could be avoided if theology had character - that is, ecclesial character!

2. Any possible interpretation of the Barmen Theological Declaration which focuses on the

present responsibility of the church has to start off with the precise meaning of the text at the time when it was formulated. This includes the analysis of its structure and of the theological intention that can be recognised in it. Attention should also be paid not only to the structure repeated in each thesis but also to the systematic slant of the six theses which interconnects and brings together all the material under a specific plan.

The theological declaration was brought about, in its own words, because "the theological presupposition" of the German Lutheran Church of the time "was constantly and fundamentally contradicted and rendered invalid." And this theological presupposition is (according to Article 1 of its constitution of 14 July 1933), "the Gospel of Jesus Christ as it is testified to us in Holy Scripture and came to light anew in the confessions of the Reformation". The Synod of Barmen had to set itself over against "the errors of the German Christians as well as... the national church government of the time which were devastating the church and destroying the unity of the German Lutheran Church."

To this end it would have been sufficient to name and reject each error. One could easily have identified and rejected them as is done in the Declaration's statements of repudiation.

9

This would have been possible following, for example, the "28 theses of the Saxon People's Church concerning the internal structure of the German Lutheran Church". These theses were unanimously accepted at the 16th Saxon Regional Synod of the Lutheran Church (with one abstention by a member of the Leipzig Faculty of Theology) and which had also been accepted beyond the Saxon Regional Church. This would have been all the more possible on account of Walter Grundmann's explanation[6] of these theses, the lucidity of which more than satisfied the wishes both of friend and foe alike. Yet at Barmen they did not understand themselves as operating in such a purely defensive way. With regard to repudiations expressed in the theological declaration, Karl Barth remarked emphatically: "The 'No' has no independent meaning."[7] In view of the errors which threatened to devastate the church and the seduction for which the Führer-church was responsible, the Barmen Declaration had something much more important to say than a mere "No". It had firstly and above all to say

[6] W. Grundmann. *Die 28 Thesen der Deutschen Christen erläutert, o. J.* [The 28 Theses of the German Christians Explained.].

[7] K. Barth, *Church Dogmatics* (eng. trans. edited by Rev. Prof. G.W. Bromiley and Rev. Prof. T.F. Torrance, Edinburgh: T&T Clark,) [hereafter *C.D.*] *II/1*, 177.

"Yes" to the one whom alone one can trust unconditionally, both in life and in death. It had first and above all to give positive expression to what evangelical[8] truth is.

For this reason positive affirmations precede the stated rejections, and, with a certainty and a joy appropriate to the situation, affirmation is given to that which they wished to see honoured as truth "in confronting errors which threatened to devastate the church". Without the affirmation of that which serves to counteract the threat to and devastation of the church, and beyond that, aids us in life and in death (for it helps to obtain eternal life); without the affirmation of the word and claim of God, revealed in the person of Jesus Christ and initiated in relation to the whole person; without an affirmation of that which the church in its visible form has to be and which the state, by divine appointment, has to do; without an affirmation of the freedom and task of the church to announce the free grace of God, the negation of those 'church-destroying' errors would in itself be groundless, weak-hearted and (since it would be without substance) ultimately ineffectual as well. The "No" has no independent meaning. It depends completely

---

[8] 'Evangelische' can also be translated 'protestant'.

on the "Yes". It can only be heard when the "Yes" is heard"[9]

The fact that this "Yes" is not a clever little theological invention, but rather a confession of the "Yes" which is spoken by God and which has become event in Jesus Christ, is brought to expression in the Barmen Declaration in that each thesis begins with God's Word itself - with a text from Holy Scripture. In this verse, as Asmussen explained before the Synod, "a whole series of verses come together" at the same time, which call Christians out of "church-destroying errors" by "demanding obedience" and calling them back to truth.[10] The quoted biblical text stands at the same time *pars pro toto* for all relevant texts but brings to speech in a particularly pointed way the evangelical truth which had to be realised in the situation at that time. And it is just this particular point, this high-point where biblical truth encounters the situation, which is brought to expression in the six articles of Barmen - first in the affirmative and then in its negative form.

[9] Ibid.
[10] Cf. *Bekenntnissynode der Deutschen Evangelischen Kirche Barmen 1934. Vorträge und Entschliessungen. Im Auftrage des Bruderrates der Bekenntnissynode*, [Confessing Synod of the German Protestant Church at Barmen, 1934. Speeches and Decisions commissioned by the Council of the Confessing Synod] published by K. Immer, 1934, 16.

The words of Holy Scripture standing at the beginning of each thesis are therefore anything but decorative quotations. They are not mottoes. Rather, they are words of address and what follows bears witness to their having been heard. Consequently the biblical texts have a pragmatic function beyond their semantic meaning: they effect those concerned and qualify their situation so that as a result it becomes possible and necessary to speak the truth. It was crucial that those who at that time confessed the evangelical truth which followed, understood themselves first as *addressed* by this truth in the form of a word of Scripture witnessing to the speaking God. In an exemplary way, Barth makes the following comment on the first of the six theses, "The force of all that is said afterwards lies in the fact that Jesus Christ has said something and indeed has said this about himself: *I* am the way and the truth and the life. *I* am the door. The church lives from the fact that she hears the voice of this "I" and grasps the promise, the sound of which is decreed to lie in this "I" alone"[11]. All the articles of the Barmen Declaration require to be understood as gathering around the One who is here saying "I" and as focusing, therefore,

[11] K. Barth, *C.D. II/1*, 177.

on Jesus Christ. Before we go into the connection and differences between the individual articles and the basic decisions formulated in them, however, it is advisable to pause and ask about the meaning of the discussion for our present time and for the task of the church today.

3. It is not easy to assert that in the evangelical church in Germany today the Gospel of Jesus Christ is being "constantly and fundamentally thwarted by foreign presuppositions and so being rendered ineffective". The present church leadership has as little to do with the government of the Reichskirche [the established church of the Reich] of that time as contemporary political theology has to do with the theology of the German Christians. *The present is not a time of church struggle.* But this well considered assessment would be terribly misunderstood if it was understood as an "all-clear" signal allowing one to sleep the sleep of the righteous. The church, as with every Christian, is "righteous and sinful at the same time", it is - to echo Vatican II - "sancta simul et semper purificanda"[12]. In this respect the church has reason to ask, continually and for all time, whether and to what extent it has thwarted

[12] Vaticanum II, Constitio dogmatica de Ecclesia "Lumen gentium", art. 8, *L. Th. K. E . I,* 174.

14

the Gospel through foreign presuppositions - so rendering it ineffective - and whether and in what form it has tolerated foreign gods in its midst. The church today has cause for extremely self-critical examination, to see whether and where such foreign gods are tolerated in its midst. It will not be possible to say that such foreign gods do their mischief in today's church *in a recognisable way*. If they are there, then they operate in the first place unrecognised, so they can do their foul work *incognito*. Far from improving the situation it would make it more dangerous if we were to commit idolatry without knowing it or noticing it. So there is not the slightest ground at all for uncritical ecclesiological self-satisfaction.

This problem, which is even less openly recognisable than the thwarting of the Gospel and the destruction of the church, cultivates itself as a rule gradually over a long period of time, to some extent gathering its momentum under the cover of the familiar. The heresy identified and fought in Barmen did not suddenly fall from heaven, but had been present for centuries as a creeping sickness in Protestantism which was unrecognised or barely recognised. Barth had already emphasised, at the Free Reformed Synod in January 1934 in Barmen, that the errors now so recognisable as destructive to the church were only the breaking out into the open of a much older fault. And in the summer of 1934 he maintained, looking back on the confession synod, that it was "not the opinion of the synod that the error against which they were turning was a novelty... We know moreover that it concerns a very old fault of the evangelical church... Today, haunted by the German Christians we are paying for the serious mistakes of faith, which were already there in our fathers and forefathers over the past centuries".[13]

So we in 1984 also have every reason to ask which faults are now eating their way to the surface in our church - and perhaps, similarly, have been unrecognised over a long time. And we also have to ask critically which problems were still not recognised by the fathers of Barmen 50 years ago or were at least not addressed by name with sufficient clarity. For example, was the church allowed to continue to treat the relationship to the Synagogue, the relationship between Christians and Jews, as a 'quantité négligeable', when shame began to be felt in Germany over the fact that Jesus had been a Jew? Instead of being satisfied with the one Lamb of God that carries the sin of the world and with his sufficiency in this respect,

[13] K. Barth, in *Texte zur Barmer Theologische Erklärung*, loc. cit. 54.

they paradoxically made "the Jews" the scape-
goat and began to send them into the worst of
all wildernesses. And may we not perhaps fall
into the opposite mistake today (through reflecting a form of self-misunderstanding in the
sense of a theological "reparation") by inter-
preting the word from the cross in such a way
that it ceases to be foolishness to the Greeks
and a stumbling-block to the Jews? That is one
of the many questions which the Barmen Declaration has given us cause to ask today. We
will come back to some other questions of this
kind in the discussion of the content of the
articles. For the time being, it is worth establishing that there may be defects that are centuries old in the evangelical church to which
our eyes must first of all be opened.

If our eyes are opened, however, then our
reactions cannot, in the light of all we have
discussed up till now, be those of mere dismissal or negation. Perhaps that is the most
significant feature of the Barmen Declaration
for us today - we must learn never to speak a
"No" without grounding it in a "Yes". For today we excel in denial and dismissal. We have
certainly learned to do that. There is not a
Sunday when we are not preached at regard-
ing what is abominable in this world, in this
state, and in ourselves as well - at least that is
how we are portrayed in the *church as institu-*

17

tion. And often that which ought to be affirmed in such dismissals and negations - if, in fact, anything at all ought to be affirmed - is nothing other than the negation of the negation, nothing other than a moral appeal on behalf of a political or quasi-political utopia. But faith lives from affirmations of a quite different kind: from affirmations which do not first arise by actualising negations and repudiations. That is, they do not arise firstly through our deeds, but precede all our doing and therefore can only be affirmed through faith - sola fide! Faith lives from the affirmation of that which God has done for us, from the affirmation that God, in that God was active for us, is there for us.

The meaning of the Barmen Declaration for the church's task today certainly consists in learning anew what is meant by, "Lo! I am with you always till the end of the world" (Matt. 28:20). It is not by chance that the final sentence of Matthew's Gospel is the beginning of the last thesis of the Barmen Declaration. Listening to this "I" means stating *positively* what is to be affirmed validly as evangelical truth in the context of a world which is increasingly setting in motion its own apocalyptic devastation. It is here, and in reality only at this point, that we can say what the church must reject in this respect. Yet as long as we are not able to say positively, by way of convincing affirmation, what the church believes to be God's promise in view of the end of the world, then the increase in the feeling of doom resulting from ecclesiastical repudiations and negations will be a serious failing in the church's task. As a mere negation it would in itself lack content, and because it is without substance it would in the end of the day be without effect. Then the church would have spoken without first having heard. Consequently, it would have failed totally to speak as the church of Jesus Christ. As church it would have spoken yet said nothing. The meaning of the Barmen Declaration for the present consists not least in reminding the church that it is only as a church listening to God's saving word, as *ecclesia audiens*, that it also has something to say.

CHAPTER 2

II

1. What the *first thesis* of the theological declaration reminds us is: to whom and to what the church must listen, and, correspondingly, what must count as the source of its knowledge and of its proclamation (as that which brings this recognition to speech). Here we will deal with it in more detail, since it is the foundational thesis for the whole Declaration, providing the other five theses with their grounding and their orientation. With this thesis the "fundamental article of the Reformation about justification through faith alone was applied to the Christian teaching of God and revelation"[14].

---

[14] "Barmen 1934/1984. Zur gegenwärtigen Bedeutung der Theogischen Erklärung von Barmen. Gemeinsamer Text aus der Evangelischen Kirche in Deutschland und dem Bund der Evangelischen Kirchen in der DDR"[Concerning the significance of the Barmen Theological Declaration for the present. Collected writings from the Protestant Church in Germany and the Federation of the Protestant Church in the DDR], in: A Burgsmüller/R. Weth (pub), *Die Barmer Theologische Erklärung. Einführung und Dokumentation.* [The Barmen Theological Declaration: Introduction and Documentation] With an introduction by E. Lohse, 1983, 81.

The first thesis does not give expression to one evangelical truth among others, but - as the preceding text from Jn 14:6 makes clear - it expresses the one and only decisive truth about the way to God and the life from God. It says that Jesus Christ alone is this truth. And it articulates this statement still more precisely, in that it claims personal acquaintance with Jesus Christ in no other way than that "in which he is witnessed to in the Holy Scripture". If *solus Christus* is to be taken seriously then it must correspond to '*sola scriptura* '. That is, if *solus Christus* is to be taken seriously, and if we are to exclude some kind of Christ-image or ideology of Christ or a Jesus-cult, some kind of heroic or social-revolutionary "Jesus Christ Superstar", or merely the scientific construct that we are accustomed to call the historical Jesus, if these are to be excluded from taking the place of the living Lord, '*solus Christus* ' must then correspond to '*sola scriptura* '.

Whoever, on the other hand, claims to be able to recognise who Jesus Christ himself is, while side-stepping Holy Scripture or, while in an unholy alliance with some other authority, whoever does this betrays him and his church. For in doing that a person has already accepted one - or more than one - foreign authority besides Jesus Christ, which will now claim, in a similar way, to provide direction and promote

21

life or even to be life-giving. Following this line one can, for example, unite the slogan 'faith in Christ, redemption through Christ, action out of Christ' with the claim that 'marriage between members of different races' must count as 'an offence against God's will', as did "The 28 theses of the Saxon People's Church"[15]. Then one can even dare - as in the declaration of intent produced by the German Christians in March 1934 - to make the claim: "... Christ, as God the helper and saviour, has, through Hitler, become mighty among us... Hitler (National Socialism) is now the way of the Spirit and Will of God for the church of Christ amongst the German nation"[16].

In thinking that one is able to get to know Jesus Christ by some means other than through the Scriptures alone, one inevitably misses Jesus Christ himself. By presuming thereby to provide guidance, promote life, or even to be life-giving, one leads people astray down disas-

[15] Die 28 Thesen der sächsischen Volkskirche zum inneren Aufbau der Deutschen Evangelischen Kirche, Thesis 27 and Thesis 5 [The 28 theses of the Saxon Peoples Church for the inner structure of the German Protestant Church, thesis 27 and thesis 5], in: K.D. Schmidt, *Die Bekenntnisse und grundsätzlichen Äusserungen zur Kirchenfrage des Jahres 1933, 1934*, [The Confessions and the Foundational Statements on Ecclesiastical Questions from the Years 1933, 1934] 99f., 102.

[16] Cf. A Burgsmüller/R. Weth (pub), loc. cit., 34.

trous, false avenues, which lead not to life but
to death. This was called euphemistically *sacri-
ficial death* and the way to it was called a "truly
heroic way of life"[17], beside which both the
cross of Jesus Christ and the National-socialist
Swastika equally stood for the ideal of sacrifice: "The Swastika is a sign of sacrifice which
lets the cross of Christ shine out for us in a
new light."[18] In view of such a statement, which
today sounds crass and primitive but which at
the time received a wide hearing, it is understandable that the Synod declared with such
sharpness, in the form of a biblical judgement:
"The one who does not go into the sheepfold
by the door but climbs in somewhere else is a
thief and a murderer" (Jn10:1). When we are
concerned with the exclusive particle 'alone',
it is, in fact, a matter of life and death - of the
way to eternal life, on the one hand, or seduction into sickness unto death on the other. It
is a matter of life and death when we must
argue about whether Jesus Christ *alone* is the
Word of God (as he alone is testified to as
such in Holy Scripture), that is, "the one we
must hear and to whom we are to trust ourselves in life and death and the one whom we
are to obey".

[17] W. Grundmann, loc. cit., 54.
[18] W. Grundmann, loc. cit., 52.

In the relative clauses quoted above it is out-
lined what *faith* means. To hear, to trust, and
to obey, are the essential elements of the Christian faith. But they are such only if it is the
Word of God become flesh and only this which
is heard; if he alone is trusted in life and death;
if this and only this Word renders one obedient and, indeed, creates obedience carried out
with pleasure and in the greatest freedom.

Of course this does not intend to contest
that we still hear many words and voices outside of this one Word of God. And this is in
no way to contest that in this life there are
both trust and things worthy of trust, obedience and that which we must obey. Indeed, it
is not even contested that there are still other
words of God outside of this one Word of God
that is Jesus Christ in person, or even that there
can be something like a natural recognition of
God. What is contested is only that such are
able to stand next to Christ and be likewise
our "comfort in life and death". What is disputed, accordingly, is that one may listen to
other words of this type within the church, so
as to claim them in like manner as sources of
that which the church must affirm and proclaim. Accordingly, this is rejected as "false
teaching", "as though the church could and
must recognise as the source of its proclamation yet other events, powers, figures, and

truths as God's revelation outside of and alongside this one Word of God".[19]

[19] The rejection clause offers a certain syntactical difficulty, in so far as the phrases "as the source of their
proclamation" and "as God's revelation" taken together
seem to make one another superfluous, or rather, they
seem to hinder one another. Erich Stanger had already
noted: "The faulty structure of the rejection clause stands
out, when the two designations, 'as the source of their
proclamation' and 'as God's revelation', appear next to
one another, without the relation between them being
defined." (Cf G. Niemöller, *Die Erste Bekenntnissynode der
Deutschen Evangelischen Kirche zu Barmen*, *pt.I* "Geschichte,
Kritik, und Bedeuutung der Synode und ihrer
Theologischen Erklärung", ["The First Confession Synod
of the German Protestant Church at Barmen, pt. 1 The
History, Criticism, and Meaning of the Synod and its
Theological Declaration"] *A.G.K. 5*, 1959, 176). The difficulty can be explained from the history of the text.
Barth's draft, the Frankfurter Konkordie, and the first
draft for the synod, did not yet have the phrase "as the
source of their proclamation". The addition of this phrase
before the second reading obviously had the function at
least of not ruling out the possibility that "still other
events and powers, forms and truths" could also be "God's
revelation". What was supposed to be ruled out was only
the ecclesial recognition of such "revelations" as sources
of the church's proclamation. Barth had already argued
similarly in *C.D. I/1*, 55f: "God can speak to us through
Russian Communism, through a flute concerto, through
a blooming bush, or through a dead dog ... God can
speak to us through a pagan or an atheist ... but we will
not be able to say that we are called to pass on as reliable
proclamation what is heard in this way", and thereby "in
practice proclaim the very persons of the heathen and
the atheist (whom one has heard) themselves".

2. In view of the meaning of Barmen for the present, it is important that the refined argumentation of the 'rejection sentence' be made clear. The only thing that is ruled out is that there are also *other sources of the church's proclamation* outside of the one Word of God, which is Jesus Christ himself. It is not ruled out that God is able to speak in many and various ways. The christocentrism of the first thesis of Barmen is not to be confused with christomonism. Indeed, this very problem, which is at least raised by so-called natural theology, is not simply denounced as an illusory problem and its possible truth denounced simply as untruth. It is important to make that clear in view of a sterile Barmen-orthodoxy! It is in no way impossible, coming from the first thesis of Barmen, and without of course practising any "natural theology", to acknowledge full well the truth of the problem of natural theology - although dealing with it in a manner quite different from the way in which natural theology itself would be able to deal with it. It is not at all impossible, coming from the one Word of God (to which alone the church has to listen, and which alone the church has to recognise as the source of its proclamation), to outline a *more natural* theology than so-called natural theology: a *natural theology* which knows Jesus Christ as the one who has reconciled both

human beings and the world (2 Cor 5:19). He is the one who, together with the prayers of Christians, also hears the groaning of the creation and who leads the children of God with the waiting creation to the redeeming *apokalypsis* (Rom 8:19-23). It is a *more natural* theology therefore, which, along with the recognition of Jesus Christ as the saviour of human beings, is learning to think anew the old notions of the salvation of phenomena (*sozein ta phainomena*). *Here* new ways open up: ways which give to each man and woman their own responsible "political theology" as well as ways which destine for each creature their own "ecological theology"!

We would have been spared a lot of foolish polemic against the Barmen Declaration if the first thesis and its rejection clause had from the outset been read and asserted with this differentiation and openness. In particular, Karl Barth, the great and inexorable opponent of so-called natural theology may be remembered in this context. Already in CD II/1 he had urged a differentiated reading of the rejection clause: "you notice that it does not deny the existence of other events, powers, images, and truths next to that one Word of God, and that it also, therefore, does not completely deny the possibility of a natural theology as such. It presupposes, moreover, that all this does in

27

fact exist. But it denies, and designates to be false teaching, the claim that all this can be the source of the church's proclamation. It excludes natural theology from the church's proclamation"[20]. There is nothing to quibble over here. This cannot be doubted. In the very exclusion from the church's proclamation of so-called natural theology, and, therefore, of ways to the heavenly Father (ways of knowledge and ways of life; that is, ways to God which go past Jesus Christ), new ways open up.

These new ways lead in the other direction moving out from this one Word of God to the world, ways to nature and to history - ways of knowledge and life which lead ever more deeply into this world as God's creation. Deeper into its needs and difficulties (*aporiai*), but also deeper into its hidden glories! Deeper, therefore, into compassionate solidarity with those who cry *de profundis* for God or perhaps no longer cry to God - who indeed, perhaps, may not even be able to cry at all in their misery. But even deeper into the joy of the unanswered mystery of the fact that we are actually here and are not rather nothing. Deeper into the joy of being able to see the one and only light of life reflecting in the manifold lights of creation and thus, in its light,

[20] K. Barth, *C.D. II/1*, 178.

being able to see with astonishment creation's own peculiar light. It was Karl Barth who in 1959 put the first thesis of Barmen - which he had formulated in 1934 - at the head of that paragraph of his *Church Dogmatics* which set out the "Glory of the Mediator" Jesus Christ, stating that the world also has "its *own* lights", indeed, "its *own* glories", "which, as such, are also their *own* words and truths"[21]. They are as "*refractions* of the one light... the lights and truths of the *theatrum* of the *gloria dei*"[22].

---

[21] K. Barth, *C.D. IV/3, First Half,* 137.
[22] Loc. cit., 152-153.

CHAPTER 3

III

1. For this reason, the objection, which was raised at the start and which has been raised again and again against the fundamental tenets of the Barmen theses - namely, that they ignore the belief in God the creator - ought to have become obsolete. The Erlangen Lutherans (but not only they) have given this objection the following form: that the Barmen Theological Declaration is a "rejection of the authority of the divine law *alongside* that of the Gospel"[23]. Furthermore, this "alongside" was, as a rule, understood in such a way that it is only through the authority of divine law that the Gospel becomes *concrete*. "Where... the person knows something of God's law, then he begins yet again to ask about the Gospel"[24]. Here the divine law is understood as the power which here and now "drives us into the bonds and orders of nature".[25] And within these natural bonds and orders the present life is deter-

[23]   W. Elert, Confessio Barmensis, in: *Allgemeine Evangelisch-Lutherische Kirchezeitung* of 29. *June 1934, No 36,* 603.

[24] W. Grundmann, loc.cit., 29.

[25]   W. Elert, loc. cit., 605.

mined concretely. The alleged, general revelation of God in the Law becomes therefore, in an underhand way, a concrete norm from which the Gospel also is supposed to acquire its concreteness from the very first. The knowledge of God as lawgiver (*cognitio Dei legalis*) understood as "general revelation" (*revelatio generalis*) becomes, *de facto, revelatio specialissima*, through which the Gospel undergoes "concretion" for the first time.[26]

In contrast to this the theology of the Barmen Declaration lives from the assumption that the revelation of God in the Gospel of Jesus Christ is concrete out of itself alone. It requires no concretion through the law. It is *revelatio specialissima et concretissima*. God's law can only be identified as God's concrete command firstly and primarily out of the *concretissimum* of the Gospel. Correspondingly, the *Second Thesis of Barmen* speaks of the fact that Jesus Christ, just as he is "God's promise of the forgiveness of all our sins, is also with the same earnestness... God's powerful claim on our whole life."

---

[26] E. Wolf, "Barmen. Kirche zwischen Versuchung und Gnade", ["The Church between Temptation and Grace"] *BzEvTh* 27, 1957, 106, has strikingly emphasised this paradox of the teaching about *revelatio generalis:* "Again and again the *revelatio generalis* becomes thus a ... *revelatio specialis*, which normalises itself *today*, and *today* is placed decisively next to the revelation of Christ."

It is of crucial significance (for the church's task today also!) that this is well and truly nailed home. For if it were otherwise, if what the Gospel has to say really only became concrete through the law, then the church would degenerate into a moral institution. The moralist lives from the fact that the accusing and convicting law holds us concretely liable. If the law were the *principium individuationis* of the Gospel, then the Gospel would not concern us *unconditionally* but only very *conditionally*. God's grace and mercy would then be abstractions which require concretion through the will of God the creator which would be perceivable through all kinds of created voices. It was in this sense that Walter Grundmann, in 1933, interpreted - with unintentional comedy - the awakening of the German people [*Volk*] as an act of God's will analogous to the creative commands of Gen.1: "Becoming a *Volk* means for us as National Socialists the fulfilment of a divine word of creation: Let there be a *Volk*! And there was a *Volk*."[27]

Before one turns up one's nose in too superior a manner here, one must ask oneself whether one does not recognise similar argumentation in our own time or, perhaps, whether one does not even argue in the same

[27] W. Grundmann, loc. cit., 15.

way oneself. How many voices within the sphere of the church or on its fringe are noticed today simply because they consider the Gospel which forgives sins as an abstraction, but they regard the law, which makes us actively involved as 'doers', as the concretissimum! The significance of the Barmen Declaration for our time ought, in a particular way, to consist in the fact that it can preserve the church from replacing the apostolic preaching of the Gospel with an *epistle of morality* - with all its demands and unattainable obligations. The apostolic succession is, however, quite the opposite of that which the moralists of all times propagate as a continued perpetration of moral rearmament.

Moralism is indeed for its part a kind of "powerful", even domineering, "demand on our whole life" - only it is not grounded in the "promise of the forgiveness of all our sins". And because of that it is, for a Christian, an absolutely unbearable demand. For only that which *liberates* our whole life may lay claim to our whole life. It is only, indeed, as our whole life is *liberated* that it ever becomes a *whole* life, a *healed* life. Asmussen was right, therefore, in inserting into Barth's draft the sentence that what encounters us through Jesus Christ is the "joyous liberation out of the godless, binding obligations of this world into free and thankful service of his creatures". This distinguishes Jesus Christ - as he claims our whole life - from all totalitarian demands, among which the moralistic demand is probably the basic model of a totalitarian claim on human life. None of these totalitarian demands liberate life. Rather, they *violate* it because they lay claim to our whole life *without* being able to *make it whole*. For the sinner has, indeed, forfeited his wholeness so that every totalitarian demand can only lead him deeper into the disintegration of his own existence. The catch is that this is consciously or unconsciously covered up under the pretence of wholeness. On this account, the Barmen Declaration, in its second thesis, has conceded a claim on our whole life to him alone who liberates this life through the "promise of the forgiveness of all our sins" and who through such liberation makes us whole. And because of this, the second thesis rejected as "false teaching", the claim that "there are areas of our life in which we belong not to Jesus Christ but to other lords, areas in which we do not need justification and sanctification through him."

2. The claims of other lords are thereby seen through and rejected as violating human life. The totalitarian claims of other lords *demand* the whole person without first being able to

grant wholeness. And, consequently, in so far as they demand the whole person, they place hopelessly excessive demands on the person in reality. At best, they forcefully integrate life which is torn into a "whole" - a "whole" which is still, in truth, the sum of many parts. These parts are often very disparate, and, without forceful integration and violating, totalitarian claims, this "whole" would immediately break up again into its parts. The moralistic violation is, in this respect, to be rejected theologically to no lesser degree than the violation by a totalitarian state ideology - whose representatives for their part take care to present themselves in the manner of an apostle of morality and in this have to be taken seriously until their immorality is proven. One cannot simply deny that those who in 1933 claimed to have recognised "the call of God to family, people, and state in the totalitarian claim of the National Socialist state"[28] meant it *morally*.

Barmen II rejected the claims of such lords in that it confessed as "evangelical truth" only the exclusive claim of Jesus Christ on our whole life. Thus the foundation was laid for an ethic of the Christian life, whose significance extended far beyond the situation at that time.

[28] W. Grundmann, loc. cit., 15.

It also goes beyond the beginnings of the Reformation without contradicting them.

3. The second thesis of Barmen has shown clearly the theological direction which determines the whole declaration. In the light of the assumption which has now been made clear - according to which the *indicative* carries the *imperative*, and the *pledge* of liberation through Jesus Christ carries his *claim* on our whole life - the remaining four theses appear as well-grounded expositions. Theses III, IV, and VI elaborate what was said previously with regard to the church: the definition of its nature and its corresponding order (Thesis III), offices (Thesis IV), and task (Thesis VI). Thesis V elaborates what was said previously with respect to the function of the state and the opposition of state and church.

CHAPTER 4

IV

The *fifth* thesis represents the Barmen version of - do not be shocked! - the Two-Kingdom-Doctrine of the Reformers. I venture this assertion, although I know that "just this thesis" stems "word for word"[29] from Karl Barth, who is to be regarded as a resolute opponent of Luther's Two-Kingdom-Doctrine. On closer examination, however, it becomes clear how very much Barth's definition of the relationship between the Christian community and the civil community is a development of the Two-Kingdom-Doctrine of the Reformers - albeit a highly original one.[30] The same goes for the fifth thesis of Barmen. It is not at all concerned only with the state, but is concerned throughout with the political existence of the Chris-

[29] K. Barth in: *Texte zur Barmer Theologischen Erklärung, loc. cit* 185.

[30] C.f. E. Jüngel, *Reden für die Stadt. Zum Verhältnis von Christengemeinde und Bürgergemeinde,* [Speaking on behalf of the City: On the relationship between the Christian community and the civil community] Kaiser Traktate 38, 1979. Also, *Zur Freiheit eines Christenmenschen. Eine Erinnerung an Luthers Schrift,* [On the freedom of a Christian. A Memorial to the Writing of Luther] *Kaiser Traktate 30,* 1978, 102-114.

tian. We would do well at the outset to exegete this Thesis (which is particularly controversial today) with recourse to the specific meaning of its words, in order to grasp the text as it was originally intended and in a manner which is as historically accurate as possible. Only then, and by way of systematic reflection, should we enquire into the significance of the fifth Barmen thesis for our present situation. Occasional repetition in this second step should be useful rather than disruptive.

A

1. First of all it is worth noting once again the *position* of the fifth thesis in the context of the theological declaration. This provides us with the first indications of the intention underlying the declaration when it comes to speak of the state.

"We would be dumb dogs if we were to set up a reformed confession without saying anything about the 'total' state". These were Barth's comments at the Free Reformed Synod at Barmen-Gemarke on the 3rd and 4th of January 1934.[31] With this remark Barth was commenting on the fact that the confession

[31] C.f. J. Beckmann, *Rheinische Bekenntnissynoden im Kirchenkampf. Eine Dokumentation aus den Jahren 1933-1945*, [The Confessing Synods of the Rhine in the Church Struggle: Documentation from the Years 1933-1945] 1975, 45.

suggested by him at that particular Synod also has something to say to the state. Since that confession by Barth was used some months later as a model in the formulation of the theological declaration, it is advisable to consult the January text as an aid in the interpretation of Barmen V. This is enlightening anyway, in view of the *position* taken in the theological declaration.

Since the sixth thesis was still missing in the draft of the "Frankfurt Concordat" finalised in Frankfurt, and originally, therefore, the fifth thesis represented the end of the whole Declaration, it may be advisable not to attach particular significance to the final, *relative* positions of the theses concerned with the form, offices, and task of the church (theses III, IV and VI). Yet, at the January Synod Barth had placed the thesis which dealt with the *state* in the context of the thesis about the *form of the church*. What is more, already at the January Synod there had been discussion of the *political experiments* of humankind under the heading *The Church In The World*. This was mentioned in the same breath as the philosophical and cultural projects of humankind, which are all "subordinated to the appointment of the divine command and the divine patience". These projects are also accompanied by the church "with its earnest recognition of its temporal, determined and limited right[,] with its intercession, but also with the reminder of God's kingdom, law, and judgement, with the hope in the One who directs everything, in order to make everything new."[32] The first version of the fifth thesis took over many of these formulations[33] throughout the various stages up to and including the text of the synod's draft, which was only formulated anew during the synod itself.

In order to understand the final version one must come to the conclusion that the thesis about the state can only be correctly understood in the context of the thesis about the church. Barmen V does not speak of the state

[32] Loc. cit., 41.
[33] The text of the model which the Synod used reads: "Scripture tells us that, by divine appointment, the state has the task of maintaining justice and security, according to the measure of human insight and human ability, under the threat and exercise of force, in the not yet redeemed world in which the church also belongs. The church, free in its being bound to its commission, accompanies with thanks and reverence towards God and with its intercession, the state, which is free in the same way in its being bound to its task, but also acts as a reminder of God's eternal kingdom, God's commandment and justice. We reject the false teaching that the state can become the single and "total" order of human life. We reject the false teaching that the church has to align itself and its message or just its shape with a particular form of state" Vgl. G. Niemöller, loc. cit., 112.

in the abstract and outside of its relations, but formulates the state's own, original and particular function as opposed to the church's own, original and particular function[34]. In relation to the background of the 'January text', one must also remember that originally implicit within the thesis about the state - at least in Barth's understanding - was the wider field of the "political, philosophical, and cultural projects of humankind", that is, everything which today is understood by the term "society". The society, no less than the state, exists in accordance with "the appointment of the divine command and the divine patience".[35]

From the beginning, Barth's intention went in a different direction from the reception and interpretation of the final version of the fifth thesis which concentrated on the authoritarian state alone. That may have been an important reason for the complaint against the ver-

[34] How F.-W. Marquardt can freely come to the claim, the "word 'state' is generally suppressed" baffles me. I find the word and its derivative occurring five times in Barmen V. Cf. F.-W.Marquardt, "Staatsbejahung oder Staatskritik? Über den Gebrauch von Barmen 5" ["Affirmation of the State or Criticism of the State? Concerning the Use of Barmen 5"] in: V.Diele (pub.), *Zumutung des Friedens. Kurt Scharf zum 80. Geburtstag, 1982,* [The Excessive Demands of Peace. On the 80th birthday of Kurt Scharf, 1982] 84.

[35] Cf. J Beckmann, loc. cit., 41.

sion of the fifth thesis presented to the synod. In complaining to the Bavarian bishop D. Meiser, Paul Althaus must have expressed the concerns of many members of the synod: "... the concept of the state which is presented here, is that of the liberal constitutional state, as in all the writings of Barth"(letter from 21.5.1934). The new version of the fifth thesis produced by Barth during the synod had taken into account such objections without thereby revoking the intention of the original version.

2. Here, also, the introductory word of Scripture definitely does not have an ornamental function but rather has a pragmatic one. The members of the synod knew themselves to be called by the Word of God to an affirmation of the state. Because of this, Asmussen, in his introductory speech, expressly emphasised "that this *one* word of Scripture binds and holds us tighter than a thousand oaths and earthly ties can hold us"[36]. Although, it must not be overemphasised, it is still noteworthy that they did not precede the text with a single word from the 13th chapter of Romans, but used, rather, 1 Pet 2:17 *pars pro toto* for the appropriate text of Holy Scripture. The context suits in

[36] Cf. *Bekenntnissynode der Deutschen Evangelischen Kirche Barmen 1934*, loc. cit., 21.

a particular way the situation of the Confessing Church, whose members - as Asmussen complained - "were suspected of being rebels"[37]. To this 1 Pet 2:15f. gives the appropriate word by suggesting that, by right action, Christians will silence the ignorance of the foolish. This they do as those who are free, but not as those who use freedom as a cover for evil. It is also noteworthy that, according to 1 Pet 2:17, God is due *fear*, as opposed to the king who is "only" due honour. The fear, which according to verse 18 determines the relationship of slaves to their masters, is obviously not the model in terms of which the relationship of Christians to their state can be appropriately understood. The apparently contradictory comments in Rom 13 relate expressly and solely to the one who does evil. "Since the government is not an object of fear for those who do good but only for the wicked"(Rom 13:3). Indeed, one is not instantly going to declare with Schiller:

"the strong bond of the law binds
only the slave mentality which scorns it".

But this much is clear: as one finds reflected in Scripture in the text of 1 Pet 2:17, under-

[37] Ibid.

stood in the light of its context, the behaviour of Christians towards the state is only described as the behaviour of people who make use of their Christian freedom (v16) when they give the state its due honour - instead of being afraid of it.

In order to understand the fifth thesis of Barmen properly one also has to pay attention to the fact that the thesis once again allows Holy Scripture to speak for itself by concluding with a final sentence from Scripture in the form of an indirect quotation. For the statement that the church trusts and obeys "the power of the word through which God maintains all things" represents an indirect quotation from Heb 1:3. According to Heb 1:3, Jesus Christ is the one who maintains all things through his powerful word: all things and therefore also the state! With the indirect quotation from Heb 1:3 in the final sentence, the church's assertions about the state are once again specifically referred back to the first thesis of Barmen. The fifth thesis would be completely misunderstood if here, of all places, the first thesis were forgotten, or if its demand were thought to be open to reduction. It is no coincidence that the final sentence takes up again the terminology of the first thesis. Moreover, when it deals with the relationship of the Christian to the state - indeed, even when it is addressing the *knowledge* of the task of the state - Christians have to listen to Jesus Christ as the one Word of God and to trust and obey him.

3. In four sentences, the thesis brings to expression what the church, as it listens to God's Word, recognises as the truth about the state and about its relationship to the state.

The first sentence formulates the task which belongs to the state according to divine ordering. The second sentence formulates the grateful affirmation by the church of the divine ordering in accordance with which the state exists and has to act. The third sentence formulates the particular task of the church with respect to the existence and task of the state. The fourth sentence once again binds the insights of the fifth thesis back to the insight of the first thesis.

It is of crucial significance for our understanding of the first sentence to see that the church operates side by side with the state: church and state both have their place "in the not-yet-redeemed-world". Obviously, it is characteristic for the not-yet-redeemed-world that state and church exist in it as two entities of very different importance. And clearly the state and the church both have their own particular functions in the not-yet-redeemed-world. In the redeemed world, however, it would no longer be necessary for the life of the human community to be represented politically on the one hand and ecclesially on the other, or, secularly on the one hand and spiritually on the other. Neither the state as such nor the church as such are created for eternity.

In the not-yet-redeemed-world the state exists because it has a worldly "task... according to divine appointment". That the state directs us back to a divine appointment (*ordinatio*) - the expression is taken from Rom 13:2 - but is not designated as an order (*ordo*) of creation, signifies a pointed disassociation from any grounding of a metaphysic of the state either in theology or natural rights. The state's existence is not an end in itself. It has no significance and no worth in itself. The state exists because and only because it has a task by virtue of divine appointment. But if it exists only in view of a particular task divinely appointed to it, then the state is bound in its existence to the divine appointment and therefore to the worldly task. Apart from this appointment and detached from this task, the state's existence would be ungrounded, its existence would not be justified. In the concept of appointment it is accentuated that the one who appoints retains constitutive significance for what is appointed. The state's responsibility before God (i.e., the responsibility of those ruling and those ruled) is intrinsic to the givenness of its existence.

The task of the state, its *raison d'être*, is very soberly defined as "maintaining justice and peace... in the not-yet-redeemed-world". Justice and peace - the previous versions had "security" instead of "peace" - are, accordingly, the goods which, in the still-unredeemed-world, are *indispensable* for human life and for life together, but which are clearly *threatened* and must be specifically safeguarded. If this care for peace and justice were not necessary, then peace and justice in the not-yet-redeemed-world would go without saying and there would be no need for the state. But peace and justice must be cared for expressly, because peace and justice in human co-existence are constantly threatened by that very co-existence.

In contrast to divine care, this care for peace and justice entrusted to the state happens "according to the measure/standard of human insight and human ability". The phrase "according to the measure" is to be understood as analogous to the phrase "according to divine ordinance". Consequently, this translates into: 'according to the measure which is given to each in the form of human insight and human ability'. Measure is here not the standard of measurement but the measurement which is accountable to the standard.[58]

Therefore "according to the measure" here is roughly equivalent to "within the framework of...", which also implies "within the bounds of...". [59] The fact that the state has to function within the bounds of *human* insight and *human* ability gives *relative* significance to its discoveries and dealings. The insights and discoveries which guide the state must be to some extent comprehensible to all people. And the very fact that they must, to some extent, be plausible to all people of their time clearly distinguishes them from the particular insights of religious communities. Whereas religious communities trace their insights back to revelation, the state is barred from doing this. Its discoveries are achieved within the boundaries of human insight. If there is nothing other than human ability alone (not least the ability of human reason) which stands at its disposal in the gaining of its insights, in the discovery

[58] The German text reads, 'Maß ist hier nicht das messende Maß, sondern das zugemessene Maß.'

[59] Correspondingly, it says in the January text that the state is the divine ordinance "in virtue of which, human beings . . . *in the framework* of their understanding of reason and history . . . have to find justice and raise themselves and maintain themselves upright". Cf. J.Beckmann, loc. cit., 45, my emphasis.

of rights, and in the definition of the nature and function of peace, then this is all the more true for the outworking of its insight. Here also the state is dealing within the bounds of human ability. None of its measures has, as such, divine dignity. None of its institutions is, as such, holy. None of its laws is the Gospel. None of its goals is a final goal. The state always acts as an agent of penultimate goals. The honour which is its due has the dignity of the second-to-last, not that of the last.

4. The means by which the state must set its insights in operation correspond to this. The Barmen Declaration names only the most extreme means: namely, "the threat and use of force". Since the state, according to the formulation of Barmen V, has to carry out its task *within a context of [unter]* threat and the use of force, yet not *by way of [durch]* threat and the use of force, one also has to reckon with other means which the state has for providing for justice and peace. The threat of the use of force is the state's *most extreme option* which accompanies all other means and is to be realised if necessary.

That it cannot remain with the *threat* of force alone, but also requires[40] the *use* of force again

[40] Barth's first outline had only "threat of force".

and again, is characteristic of the not-yet-redeemed world within which the state has to act
in a way which is different from that of the
church. The church operates through the power
of the Word (*sine vi, sed verbo*) by placing its trust in
the power of the Word by which God sustains all
things. The state, on the other hand, is dependant
on the use of force in order to put its insights into
practice, and to be able to achieve this with respect
to everyone. Indeed, both church and state have
to do with sinful people. The church has the spiritual task of proclaiming the sin-forgiving justice of
God and therefore to forgive the sin of the sinner
in the name of God, in order thus to urge one to a
sinless life. The state, however, has to work in worldly
ways against sin in its worldly forms, and that means:
within the context of threat and, if necessary, also
within the context of the use of force.

There is a standpoint which is not to be
disputed and which suggests that it is precisely
this way of using force which tempts the state
on its part to sin by perverting what is a means
into an end in itself. Here, the use of force
comes to be conceived as belonging almost to
the *essence* of the state.[41] However, this ought

[41] Barth stressed that it did not belong to the essence
of the state to exercise force: "...force does not belong to
the *opus proprium* but to the *opus alienum* of the state." K.
Barth, in: *Texte zur barmer Theologischen Erklärung*, loc.
cit., 197; cf. also *C.D. III/4*, 456.

not to obscure the primary point which is the following: the state only has the monopoly on force for the sake of its task, which consists in looking after justice and peace. It is for this and for this purpose alone that it is ordained by God. It is for this and for this purpose alone that the state is entrusted with the means of force.

Therefore the state cannot really be an object of fear as well. Moreover, the church recognises "in thanks and reverence before God the benevolence of this God's appointment". The second sentence of the fifth thesis formulates the church's attitude with respect to the state in such a way that the church turns firstly to God. It recognises in the divine ordering an act of benevolence, which corresponds to the state's obligation to maintain justice and peace. And it recognises this benevolent act significantly in thanks and reverence before God, not in thanks and reverence before the state. The state is a benevolent provision because it serves humanity in its care for justice and peace. In this statement Barmen V is in harmony with the *Confessio Augustana* which had designated the *legitimae ordinationes civiles* as the *bona opera Dei* (CA 16).

It is noteworthy that there is a remarkable difference between the original outlines and the final form of the statement. The previous versions spoke of the church - in its being bound to its task - as free. As such it stands together, in and through its intercessions, with the state which is equally free in its being bound to its task. We have already noted that talk of the free church in the free state[42] reminiscent of Cavour, provoked Lutheran concerns. Obviously, they did not want the state to become locked into the form of the liberal, constitutional state. Therefore, the text had to be reformulated. It is absolutely unbelievable that the intercession of the church for the state, which had been strongly emphasised in the previous versions, was left out in the new formulation. For, in intercession, the church takes on the worldly task of the state in a spiritual way. In intercession, the church shares the state's concerns. Inasmuch as mention of the state's being accompanied by the interceding church is erased without replacement, the final formulation of the fifth thesis presents *no* improvement on the previous versions.

5. The third clause formulates the attitude of the church vis-a-vis the state in such a way that both those currently ruling and their subjects

---

[42] This is how Barth formulated it in the text of the January Confession. Cf. J. Beckmann, loc. cit., 45.

are addressed. Significantly, however, this does not happen by way of the church becoming directly political and then trying to improve by political means those things which the state has either done poorly (whether supposedly or actually) or has threatened to do. Rather, the church speaks both to those who rule and their subjects by reminding them "of God's kingdom and of God's commandment and righteousness". *"Thereby"* it reminds them "of the *responsibility* of those who rule and those ruled". Responsibility in the realm of the political implies a being-drawn-into-responsibility by God, who (with the promise of his coming kingdom, the instruction of his commandments and the establishing of his justice) provides human insight with the *criteria* by which political activity is to be measured. If the church serves to remind those ruling and those ruled of their responsibilities by reminding them of God's kingdom, commandment and righteousness - as that involves returning to its proclamation and instruction - then it contributes in its own way (which, although indirect, cannot be overlooked) to the state's maintenance of justice and peace in accordance with human insight and human capabilities. Consequently, there exists, despite all the differences, a positive relationship between the task of the church and the task of the state, which we shall have to examine in more detail by systematic discussion.

The phrase 'those who rule and those who are ruled' may have been interpreted in a rather one-sided manner by the members of the synod at that time - along the lines that those who rule have and "take responsibility", whereas those who are ruled, on the other hand, "are held responsible". But the wording of the thesis includes both the rulers and the ruled in a common responsibility. This common responsibility originates not least from the fact that in God's kingdom, and before God's commandment and righteousness, all are equal. By being a reminder of God's kingdom, commandment, and righteousness, the church lays the theological foundation for the Christian's political existence.

The fourth clause connects with Barmen's first thesis by way of its indirect quotation from Scripture. It brings to expression the fact that the church knows that the state is also grounded in, and sustained by, the power of God's Word. The state, which has to serve the preservation of life by maintaining justice and peace, is, for its part, contingent upon its preservation through God's Word. Thereby, every claim to omnipotence by the state is clearly contradicted, but contradicted by a *promise* which is also valid for the state. If it exists by virtue of divine ordering then the church can trust and obey - even with regard to the state - the power of the Word by which God sustains all things.

6. Barmen V closes with a two-fold rejection. The terminology of rejection makes it clear that in the relationship of the church to the state and of the state to the church, a *status confessionis* can also arise which makes it necessary to designate false teaching unambiguously. The first rejection refers to a false, religious self-understanding by the state, and the second rejection refers to a false, political self-understanding by the church. Both false self-understandings condition one another inasmuch as a state which misunderstands itself in a religious way seduces the church to a false political self-understanding, and a church which misunderstands itself politically, in turn, simply impresses a religious self-understanding on the state. As "false teachings", however, such false self-understandings can only be rejected, if, in any way, they appear as teaching of the church or if they try to penetrate the church's teaching.

The first rejection clause draws out the consequences of the first and second Barmen thesis for the content of the fifth thesis. Is Jesus Christ the one Word of God whom we have to trust and obey in life and in death? Is he God's

powerful claim on our life? If so then it is
"false teaching" when it is maintained that the
state "should and can,... over and above its
special commission, be the single and total order of human life and fulfil in addition, therefore, the purpose of the church". The totalitarian claim of the state, which was approved
and theologically grounded by the German
Christians, and by other theologians as well,
and which sought to order human life completely and in every respect (thereby exclud-
ing other interests and claims), is identified
and rejected as a religious encroachment. In
this case, such a claim by the state is bound to
lead to the desire to fulfil the purpose of the
church as well. Precisely by virtue of its being
untrue to its real purpose the state fails in its
special task, and instead violates justice and
creates discord in the form of acts of quasi-
religious pacification. The totalitarian claim of
the state makes life necessarily *one-dimensional*
and is thereby already devoid of the true meaning of peace and justice. One-dimensional
peace is graveyard[43] peace. One-dimensional
justice is the justice of the strongest.

The second rejection clause draws out the
same consequences but this time with regard
to the church. If the state does not have any

[43] Lit. 'peaceyard'.

56

claim to fulfil the purpose of the church, then the church must stand over and against it in its own 'unexchangeable' identity. Consequently, it is to be rejected as "false teaching that the church can and should go beyond its own special responsibility by acquiring the characteristics, functions and dignities of the state, thereby becoming itself an organ of the state". Asmussen stressed before the synod that the church is bound by the Gospel - exists "in the sphere of the Gospel" - which rules out the church itself becoming a political legislator. Thereby it would not only overstep "its borders", but in so doing it would drag "the state down with itself into its own mire".[44] The church owes it to itself, as well as to the state, to be able to distinguish between its being bound to the sphere of the Gospel and the specific binding of the state within the sphere of the law. The church is under the same obligation constantly to make this distinction anew.

In this first 'run-through' we have ascertained the literal sense of the fifth Barmen thesis and explained it briefly. The author of this text later described it as the "minimum" of that "which the community for the sake of the faith... had to say, and also what the com-

---

[44] Cf. *Bekenntnissynode der Deutschen Evangelischen Kirche Barmen 1934*, loc. cit., 22.

munity just managed to say - in a context of
extreme urgency and by summoning up all its
courage while, at the same time, being afflicted
from the outside and lacking any united political orientation. We were just not a very
strong and very lively church"[45]. That is why
the fifth Barmen thesis cannot be seen as a
maximal expression of what the church should
be able to say about its relationship to the state
following the end of the National Socialist tyr-
anny. But is it not perhaps the case that a
community which is under very much less af-
fliction from the outside is still less in a position to prove itself worthy of its freedom for
the Word? At any rate we will do well at least
to keep to that minimum, which the Christian
community in a more difficult time held in its
confession to be unrenouncable. For that reason we shall now inquire systematically into
the meaning of the text, exegetically explained,
for our own situation.

B.

The special significance of this particular text
for the present time consists, first of all, in the
fact that the thought and expression here were

---

[45] Karl Barth in : *Texte zur Barmer Theologischen
Erklärung*, loc. cit., 169.

in the tradition of the insights of the Reformation - as they were in the first thesis. The result of this is that the *solus Christus* clause was used to advantage in addressing the question of the source of theological understanding, as it was in the first thesis. This was now of much greater consequence, however, than it was at the time of the Reformation. The relationship of church and state is thought through here in a more powerful way than the Reformers had done, in that the authors of the Barmen Confession thought 'out of' the fact that Jesus Christ is the Word of Power (Greek: *rhema tes dunameos*) by which God maintains all things and therefore also the state. Indeed, not only did the theology of the Reformation not deny this in principle, but actually asserted it in a basic form. But this was, indeed, only in a basic form in that Barth, in view of the positive, theological relationship between political power and the power of Christ, between justice and justification, could remark that "the interests of the reformational confessions of faith and, in general, of reformational theology stopped or at least weakened" just at that point where it ought properly to have begun.[46] In the fifth

[46] Karl Barth, "Rechtfertigung und Recht", *Th.St. 104*, 1970, 5f.

Barmen thesis, however, the New Testament truth of "the power of the word, through which God maintains all things", is to be recognised as a basis for a christological foundation of the state. "This final sentence... with its christological foundation of the state has no doubt missed out on its fair share of the discussion in the decades since Barmen. Not everyone has noticed what is actually said in this sentence, which, at least for me as the one who suggested it at the time, was the centre," as Barth commented later.[47]

And in actual fact, if "Fear God!" and "Honour the king!" are meant to be in harmony, and if it is the case, therefore, that we, in our self-understanding as citizens, ought not to disregard the fact that we are called to a citizenship in God's coming kingdom and, furthermore, if the responsibility of the rulers and those ruled is sharpened and ultimately grounded in the reminder "of God's kingdom, law and righteousness", then in the midst of the difference between church and state, between faith and politics, there must be a positive relationship between both sides. Scripture then must also have something to say to us in this respect.

[47] K Barth, in: *Texte zur Barmer Theologischen Erklärung,* loc. cit., 190.

1. In any case, according to Barmen V, there is already a positive relationship between state and church, in that both state and church have to carry out their responsibilities "in the not-yet-redeemed-world". Indeed, the very fact that the state and the church are two different things, that the human community exists in this *duality* of a political and a spiritual community, and, therefore, that the church faces the state as something very special - that very fact is especially *indicative* of the world which is indeed reconciled in Jesus Christ but remains as yet unredeemed. The church will exit and make room for the coming *polis* when humanity is liberated from living in a "not-yet-redeemed-world". Then Christian existence will be directly identical with political existence. Then life in the *polis* will be unambiguously Christian (i.e., a life in accordance with God). Then, finally!

In the not-yet-redeemed-world, however, the church is in *solidarity* with the state, precisely in that it stands over and against it as a community *sui generis*. It is the first and fundamental act of the church's *loyalty* towards the state, that it *differentiates* as strictly as possible between church and state. It remains faithful to the state when it denies the state any religious dignity and every worthiness to be worshipped, and reminds it that God alone is to be worshipped. "In the state nothing and no-one is to be worshipped"[48]. Our intercessions are - importantly enough! - meant for the state, but our worship is not. And the intercession for the state makes it clear that it does not exist and operate out of its own absolute power, but is there "according to divine ordination" for the fulfilment of quite specific tasks. The concept of the divine appointment (*ordinatio*), which has been deliberately chosen instead of the concept of order (*ordo* - which can be interpreted in the sense of orders of creation), makes clear for its own part that there are limits set for the state. And one limit, if not the decisive limit, is set for it in that the church stands over and against it "in the not-yet-redeemed-world". By doing this, it protects the state from a religious or quasi-religious self-misunderstanding and thereby serves it in the best possible way. For a state which misunderstands itself religiously or quasi-religiously, rather than being the deacon and servant of God in accordance with Rom. 13:4-6, degenerates into the beast from the abyss envisaged in Rev. 13. "If the state announces an eternal kingdom [*Reich*], an eternal law and an eternal justice [*Gerechtigkeit*], then it corrupts itself and

---

[48] E. Jüngel, *Reden für die Stadt*, loc. cit., 29.

its people along with it," Asmussen declared to the synod in view of the "thousand-year" Reich.[49] Therefore, the church exercises its faithfulness towards the state when it rejects as "false teaching" the claim "that the state can and should go beyond its special responsibility to become the single and total order of human life and thus also to fulfil the purpose of the church".

2. Conversely, however, the church remains true to itself as well, by taking good care not to take the place of the state. The church knows, and Holy Scripture tells it, that the state not only has to carry out its own task, but also has to do so "by the threat and use of force". And there is never any situation where this becomes the business of the church. It has to display *divine* law effectively, and that happens "without human force and by God's Word alone: *sine vi humana, sed verbo*" (CA 28)[50]. Therefore, the church will not be allowed to slip into the mistake of considering whether it might take the place of the state, in order thereby to do better what the state supposedly - or even actually - does badly or less well. With

[49] Cf. *Bekenntnissynode der Deutschen Evangelischen Kirche Barmen 1934*, loc. cit., 22.
[50] *BSLK 124*, 4 ff.

such presumptuousness the church would do more than merely involve itself in something that is not its business, that is, which it is not permitted to do according to CA 28.[51] With such presumptuousness the church would even deny the state precisely that which the Holy Scriptures promise it: namely to be able to function "according to divine appointment" and therefore to represent a benevolent act of God. Whoever questions this, by word or deed, is working for a demonisation of the state. Whoever, by thought, word, or deed, denies that the state, by carrying out its responsibilities (whether it knows it or not), operates according to a benevolent arrangement of God, dispenses those ruling and those ruled of their responsibility before God. It is the devil himself who gives out this dispensation and irresponsibly carries out his mischief. One must be careful not to understand the state according to his, that is the devil's, image! Like every religious deification, every demonisation of the state is also a thoroughly unchristian undertaking.[52]

[51] *BSLK 122*, 25 f.

[52] Cf. K. Barth, "Rechtfertigung und Recht", [Justification and Justice] loc. cit., 27: "The opposite of such idolatry, which would consist to a certain degree in a demonisation of the state, is impossible, however, ... Not because its representatives, bearers and citizens could

If the church does not want to presume to take the place of the state, then it will also not presume to want to become a political legislator. By doing this it would again "slip into involving itself in something that is not its business". Worse still, it would distort beyond recognition its own particular task if it were to confuse or mix the proclamation of the Gospel with political legislation. Therefore, Barmen V also rejected as "false teaching" the idea "that the church could and should expand beyond its particular task to take on the characteristics, functions and dignity of the state and thereby become itself an organ of the state". There is nothing to be added to that today.

3. But up to this point we have not paid any attention to the way in which the particular *content* relating to the task of the state, and the church's proclamation in this regard, is defined in Barmen V. But whether the matters discussed in principle up to this point achieve a *concrete meaning* depends on the actualisa-

not protect" the *civitas terrena* "from actually becoming the state of Cain or even of the devil, but rather, because even the heavenly Jerusalem is a *state*, even the worst and most disarrayed earthly state has within it its everlasting purpose to contribute to the magnificence of the heavenly Jerusalem or in some way to bring its tribute there".

tion of these definitions of content. What is *concretely* at stake here is the relationship between church and state, which until now has been discussed from the point of view of their differentiatedness *in principle*. Indeed, it must be proven *in concreto* that the *right differentiation* between church and state means a *positive co-ordinating* and not an *indifferent co-existence*. An abstract relationship of Christians to political existence would be a terrible misunderstanding of the distinction between state and church discussed thus far.

For that which the state is obliged to safeguard concretely (in all the *differentiatedness* of heavenly and earthly *politeuma*), remains a *simile* of that for which Christians hope, in that they hope for God's coming heavenly kingdom. Indeed, here we come up against one of the most important problems of theological ethics. *The mere naming* of concepts, like peace and justice, in no way determines *what* the state has to maintain in practice. Rather, it is necessary to enquire *into the truth* of these concepts. What in truth deserves to be called peace and justice is definitely not immediately certain. It was not at all obvious in 1934, and at no time has it been settled beyond dispute, *what* the concepts of peace and justice mean in substance. From 1933 onwards you could find general and widespread approval in Germany of

the slogan that justice is what serves the people, and what serves the people is determined
by the party or the Führer, who "by virtue of his
leadership is the sole architect of justice as its
highest judge... From the leadership flows justice".[53] One can still find the same slogan in
force today (albeit with slight variations) in a
number of states serving, either officially or se-
cretly, as the axiom of jurisdiction. And at
present we are experiencing a dispute about
the concept of peace, in which opposing
understandings of peace policy exist in conflict
with one another - a situation which is caused
largely by different definitions of the concept's
content.

What in truth deserves to be called peace,
justice and righteousness (one could add 'freedom'!) is by no means, therefore, decided. This
means that all these political concepts are *lacking truth.* For Christians, their lack of truth
necessarily calls theology into the arena. If a
political dimension is necessarily a part of
Christian existence, then the church and theology cannot just stand aside and observe with-

[53] C.Schmidt, "Der Führer schützt das Recht" [The
Führer protects Justice] (on the 30th June1934), in: *Der
Nationalsozialismus. Dokumente 1933-1945.* [National Socialism. Documents 1933-1945] Published with a com-
mentary by W. Hofer, Nr. 55, 105.

out being involved. This is precluded if we are obliged to come to a decision on the meaning of the basic, political concepts of peace and justice, and thereby to decide what the state has to do in practice when it has to provide for peace and justice "according to the measure of human insight and human ability".

The measure (or standard) of human insight is not an absolute rule for the church. Rather, it is a rule which itself is to be measured against the yardstick of Holy Scripture. Because of this, the church "reminds" those ruling and those ruled "of God's kingdom, God's commandment and righteousness". In this way, it confronts the political concepts lacking in truth with the truth-claim of faith. And it achieves its contribution to the definition of these political concepts within the bounds of human insight by serving as a reminder, for example, that God's righteousness is a righteousness which justifies the sinner, thereby attaching *inviolable value to the human person* whose worldly protection must be expressed in a number of *human rights* which ought to be introduced into every constitution.[54] Correspond-

---

[54] Cf. E. Jüngel, "Freiheitsrechte und Gerechtigkeit" [Justice and the Rights of Freedom], in: *Unterwegs zur Sache*, 1972, 246-256. W. Huber/H.E. Tödt, *Menschenrechte. Perspektive einer menschlichen Welt*, [Human Rights. Perspectives on a Humane World], 1978.

ingly, because of this reminder of God's kingdom and commandment, one is obliged to enquire what it actually means "to maintain justice and peace". In the process, however, one
will always have to bear in mind that the command of God and the law of the state, the
kingdom of God and the socio-political structure of the state, are different and must remain distinguishable. Only then can the
church and what it remembers provide a historically meaningful contribution to the definition of these political concepts and their fea-
sibility within the bounds of human insight.
This becomes immediately clear when we com-
pare the Christian hope of the kingdom of
God on the one hand with the actual condition of existing states, and our hope of their
improvement, on the other.

What then are we hoping for? What are we
expecting when we expect the Kingdom of
God? The Bible tells us that, in God's coming
kingdom, peace and justice *kiss one another* and
therefore no longer stand apart, so that this
inner connection between peace and justice
cannot even be conceived without joy in the
Holy Spirit (Rom 14: 17; cf. Ps 85:11). This is
not the case here on earth. Here peace and
justice are not self-evident. Not even the in-
tensive fellowship of peace and justice which
has happily been brought to expression

through the metaphor of the kiss is self-evident in our earthly life. Therefore in regard to the earthly *polis* there can be no talk of joy in the Holy Spirit. It is for precisely this reason that the state must concern itself specifically with peace and justice and do so "according to the measure of human insight and human possibility by deterrent means" and *ultima ratione* "by way of the use of force".

4. But this gives all earthly kingdoms and all earthly politics an inevitable ambivalence and ambiguity. It is only God's coming kingdom that is distinguished by unambiguity, for in it life will be formed and ordered in accordance with the measure of *divine* insight and *divine* ability. And the essence of both divine insight and divine ability is the mystery of divine love which makes everything unambiguous. At the heart of divine wisdom and might reigns love as its solid core. That, however, is not something that can be said simply and without hesitation out of our insight and our ability. In this context, it is by no means only love that reigns. But with love the unambiguity of life invariably disappears as well. In political life on earth one has to make compromises, but if, after all, the compromise fails, one has to threaten with force and, if necessary, use it. That is why justice on earth requires, very sadly,

the existence of prisons. One must be aware of this ambivalence and ambiguity as it relates to all political actions. Indeed, one has to affirm them. In no way does this detract from the value of political activity, for by providing for peace and justice in its own problematic way the state is still, at least allegorically, related to that which Christians proclaim and expect as God's unambiguous kingdom.

For this reason Christians, and also the church - in the proclamation of the Gospel of God's coming kingdom - possess *criteria*, by way of God's command and God's justice-creating righteousness, for that which is to be established in the earthly state as justice and peace. As we have already said, the church will not, thereby, become an active law-giver itself. It will not pervert the Gospel, which liberates from godless bonds, by reducing it to law and thereby making it ambiguous. And, in the same way, it will not pervert the political work of the legislator, the executive, and the earthly courts by making cumbersome and dubious demands on their use of power (which is necessarily problematic, ambivalent and ambiguous) by introducing the unambiguous claims of the kingdom of God. But it will bring to bear on the legislator *strenuous demands* from the Gospel, *strenuous,* evangelical *demands*, which serve as criteria for that which (within the limits of human insight) is to be regarded as earthly justice and earthly peace and for that which is to be put in operation, albeit within the limits of human ability.

And, above all, it will demand from every individual Christian an awareness of political responsibility. That the state (which Barmen V viewed in rather over-authoritarian terms) consists of rulers and those ruled, cannot, however, obscure the fact that the state is nothing other than the form of the political life of its citizens. We are the state! Therefore, one cannot speak of the state without at the same time speaking of the society which makes it possible, and for whose well-being it is responsible. This must be held together with the other institutions and effective elements within society.[55] That is a starting-point for *critical* debate with the fifth thesis of Barmen.

[55] W. Huber (*Folgen christlicher Freiheit*, [Consequences of Christian Freedom] loc. cit.), appealing to H. Ehmke, "'Staat' und 'Gesellschaft' als verfassungstheoretisches Problem" ['State' and 'Society' as a Problem for Constitutional Theory], in: *Staatsverfassung und Kirchenordnung. Festschrift für R. Smend,* [The Constitution of the State and the Order of the Church: *Festschrift* for R. Smend]1962, 23 ff, rightly refers to the fact that "the state..." can "no longer be thought of as a sovereign power independant of society". "Rather this one, in the structure of its pre-democratic conception of the state is superseded by another, which conceives of the state as

Together with this there arises a second critical remark. If the church, with its proclamation of the Gospel and with its talk of the kingdom of God, is thereby a reminder of God's command and God's righteousness (just as the ambivalence and ambiguity of earthly political existence corresponds, at least allegorically, to the heavenly *politeuma* - and can thereby become an analogue), then one certainly must put the critical question to Barmen V as to why the additional task of providing for *freedom*, within the limits of human insight and human ability, is not expressly demanded here of the state. The power of the Gospel to liberate from godless bonds sheds some light upon the political realm. Karl Barth later regretted that, in formulating the fifth thesis, he did not, in addition, demand expressly of the state the responsibility for safe-guarding freedom. "Actually that word should have been resounding even then, in 1934: the word freedom... freedom understood... (as) the personal responsibility of all."[56]

---

the form of the political self-organisation of the society... That which the theological tradition calls 'authority' is encountered today on very different levels and in different forms...". All the same, the church does not only exist in democratic societies!

[56] K. Barth, in: *Texte zur Barmer Theologischen Erklärung,* loc. cit., 200.

5. Finally, if we are inquiring about the meaning of the Barmen Declaration for the task of the church today, there is one more critical difficulty which requires discussion. What does it mean today, in 1984, that the state has the task of providing for *peace*, "within the limits of human insight and human ability, by means of the threat and use of force"? Can the threat and use of force still mean today the threat and use of weapons of war, as they had tacitly assumed in 1934 following the consensus of previous centuries? [57] Rather, is it not the case that the church today, by reminding of God's kingdom, God's command and God's justice, has to address an urgent demand to the legislator to renounce permanently the threat and use of armed force? With this question we come up against a problem which is contested today in a particularly passionate way, indeed one which is straining the unity of Christians to breaking point. Therefore, I want to speak

[57] After all, Otto Dibelius of all people had already in 1930 pleaded "for the general disarmament of the people" and declared: " without an *if* or a *but*, without qualification [*Einschränkung*] and compromise... [:] war ought not to be, because God does not desire war." Cf. O. Dibelius, *Friede auf Erden? Frage, Erwägungen, Antwort, 1930 (3)*, [Peace on Earth? Questions, Considerations, Answer, 1930 (3)]18f. 212 ff.

74

in a particularly peaceable way, but also as unambiguously as possible; that is, with the passion of patience which knows only one opponent: theological confusion. Indeed, in order
to counter this confusion formally, I shall subject this point to a further subdivision.

a) Today, the question of the legitimacy of
the threat and use of military force is generally treated in such a way that it is applied only
to the threat and use of force as this involves
nuclear weapons. And then it is popular to
argue that, within the limits of human insight,
the use of such weapons would destroy the
very life, and its conditions, which this threat
and use of force is obliged to protect. Therefore, one may neither threaten with, nor deto-
nate, nuclear weapons. At the moment not only
are the various actions of the Christian peace
movements (with whose goals I largely identify myself) grounded in such argumentation,
but today the possibility of resistance against
the force of the state is dependent on it as
well. Yet not only do I consider this argumentation a dangerous constriction, but I also consider it extremely problematic for this reason:
it seems to suggest that deterrence and the
use of military force *without nuclear weapons* is
theologically justified. Such argumentation is,
quite simply, theologically untenable. Moreo-

75

ver, it is essentially not a *theological* but a *purely political* form of argument.

What is lacking in the diverse activities of the Christian peace movement, as these are manifest in its resistance against the possibility of the world's destruction through war, is exactly that which (in my opinion) the church opposition of the years 1933 and 1934 was lacking prior to the Barmen Synod. What it "lacked" at that time was "the recognition that the issue really concerned faith", as Barth had already stated in 1934 with the purpose of posing the question: "... if there is a lack of recognition... that it was really a matter of faith, how could fighting be just and necessary?".[58] For on the basis of political "motives, one could not, and cannot, speak in the name of the church."[59] In a parallel way today, there is also a lack of a clear *understanding of faith*, which can be transformed into the strict language of a *confession of faith*, because there is a fixation with the political controversy as to whether nuclear weapons may or may not be used as a deterrent.

[58] K. Barth, in: *Texte zur Barmer Theologischen Erklärung.* loc. cit., 33.
[59] Loc. cit., 31.

A *confession of faith* of this type is somewhat different from a *political calculation*. Indeed, it has to perceive and consider carefully the political situation to which it is obliged to speak, and the political knowledge which is available. But if it is to be a *confession of faith*, it will certainly not allow itself to be forced into *formulating questions in political ways*. And in so far as the confession of faith has, and must have, political consequences, the corresponding, strenuous demands must in this respect be evangelical; that is, they must be strenuous demands obtained through the recognition of the Gospel. Therefore, when the church comes to a *confession of faith* in relation to the question of the boundaries of deterrence and the use of force (with recourse to which the state has to provide for peace), it has, in this matter also, no other authority than that pertaining to a request. It makes its request in Christ's place (2 Cor 5: 20). This is somewhat different from resistance against a state whose government is freely chosen and which must submit again to election by its citizens. One has to deal with the concept of resistance against the state extremely carefully, for the very reason that this could one day be called for by the Gospel. For Christians in the Federal Republic of Germany today, it is only the apostolically authorised renunciation of the threat and use

77

of military force which comes into considera-tion.[60] I would describe such precautionary and timely resistance not as being against the state but in the interests of the state, properly un-derstood. But this type of thing is also only *possible* for Christians if and when it is *called for* through that insight which belongs to faith. Does faith provide such insight? Can we ob-tain it?

b) The political fact of which the Confes-sion of Faith must be cognisant, and to which consideration must be given, is doubtless this: through the existence of nuclear weapons and the knowledge of their capacity for mass-ex-termination - indeed, global destruction - our eyes have been opened anew to what it means

---

[60] To think that the possibility of using atomic war-fare must completely discredit the power of the state, and what is more, must cause the church to legitimate no longer the state's right to threat and the use of force and cause it to reject any similar notions, is according to F. W. Marquardt (loc. cit., 99), to throw the baby out with the bath water. If it is also the case that the use of force is in no way the *opus proprium* of the state, then the recognition of the divine appointment of the state is certainly not conceivable without the affirmation of force as the *opus alienum* of the state in the not-yet-redeemed world. Marquardt's option means a theological abdica-tion in that the question of the limitation of the state's force is no longer allowed to be posed at all. Those who desire the impossible thereby threaten to make every-thing possible - even what they do not desire.

to make war. With this new quality of understanding which our human insight possesses, the already obvious question ought now to force itself irrefutably upon the church: namely, whether its being reminded of God's kingdom, God's law and God's righteousness would at any time have made it permissible to be at war. The political dilemmas of a consequent refusal of military service are obvious. It still remains to be seen whether these dilemmas are more severe (or not, rather, significantly less severe) than the dilemmas in which the threat of armed force is already entangling itself. Nevertheless, the first case poses dilemmas as well. And it would be dishonest to argue against that or to minimise it. However, I certainly regard the necessary political consideration here to be an extremely important problem, although a subordinate one.

The paramount question - paramount in that it concerns a *theological* problem of the first order - is the question as to whether the church will not have its eyes opened, by way of the new degree of weaponry, to the fact that, precisely by virtue of its being the church, it must identify every war as mocking the kingdom of God which it must proclaim, as trespassing the command of God which it must proclaim, and as perverting the righteousness of God which it must proclaim. It is the obligation of the church to remind those who rule and those who are ruled *of all this* by reminding them of their *responsibility* before God. Consequently, is it not the case that the church must admit that it has for centuries sustained a heresy inasmuch as it has conceded the possibility of a just war and also of a war justified by God?[61] Must not the church itself first do theological penance if it recognises itself as being committed to continue thinking along the lines of Barmen in 1984? Must it not return to the insight, which was once alive in earliest Christianity, that one cannot both believe in God and *desire* to be a warrior?[62] Is it not the case that, contrary to what is valid today, the one who is prepared to take up weapons, whose purpose is deterrence and the use of military force, is obliged at least to proffer express reasons of conscience for doing this?

---

[61] Cf. *CA 16*: "liceat . . . iure bellare" (*BSLK 70*, 11 ff); cf. Apol. to *CA 16*: " Since it is God's work, . . . if one . . . makes war for the sake of the common peace " (*BSLK 309*, 29 ff).

[62] Cf. Hyppolyte's Church order, canons 14, 74; 13, 14, in: *La Tradition Apolostique de Saint Hippolyte. Essai de Reconstitution par Dom B. Botte O.S.B.*, [The Apostolic tradition of Saint Hippolyte, A reconstructive essay by Dom B. Botte O.S.B.], *L.W.Q.F. 39*, 1963, 36, 12 f: "Catechumenus vel fidelis qui volunt fieri milites reiciantur, quia contempserunt (Gk. *kataphronein*) deum."

I am aware of the suspicions to which one exposes oneself - in *all parts* of the world and therefore, in *both* parts of Germany, I might add - if one dares to raise questions of this sort. I know that, in particular, the high value of a liberal democracy could stand in opposition to this kind of questioning. This is also for me a high, indeed a very high, value which is worth defending. But do we do so by way of the threat and use of military force? That is *the question.* In any case, I could no longer - *magis amica veritas!* - be a teacher of the church today without asking this question.

Its *answering* requires not only spiritual bravery but also intellectual honesty. For this reason, we must make the answering of this question as difficult as possible for ourselves. We shall have to find greater clarity if, on a matter of such major importance, we are not to replace with some "tidy little theological creation" that which the church itself must first be called to remember and of which further it must remind both society and the state.

c) First of all, we shall have to make it quite clear that the "threat and use of force" is indeed part of the *means* by which the state has to provide for peace, but that it is certainly not the only *means* which the state possesses by which to provide for peace. The same applies to justice. At least with regard to internal politics, the state has first of all to provide for peace by radically different means from those involving force. Were that the only means then peace would be - in Thomas Hobbes' sense - nothing other than the state of non-violence [*Gewaltlosigkeit*] amongst its citizens reached by means of the violence [*Gewalt*] of the state. And, with regard to external politics, peace would be - precisely in the sense of the Pax Romana - the interruption of what is in actuality a natural state of war: an interruption which can only come by force and can only be maintained by force.[63] On the contrary, if the concept is to be defined with reference to its biblical use, peace is the successful 'being-whole' (shalom) of one's life and therefore of the living, political community. The successful being-whole of the political living community is, however, not only to be defended by force against violent destruction, but it is first of all *to be built up* and then continually *built up*. Social provision and care, for example, are much more appropriate means for this than the threat and use of force.

d) We will then have to make it clear that the *means* of the state are not to be confused

---

[63] Cf. E. Jüngel, *Zum Wesen des Friedens. Frieden als Kategorie theologischer Anthropologie*, [On The Essence of Peace. Peace as a Category of Theological Anthropology], *Kaiser Traktate 74*, 1983, 18.

with the *definition* of the state. The state is defined by the fact that it has to look after justice and peace - and we ought now to add, therefore - freedom. The threat and use of force may be a necessary *means* to that but it does not *define* the state. Therefore, it is extremely important here to be absolutely clear about this distinction, because the use of force does indeed endanger peace. For this very reason, (i.e., because of this use of force), the state must safeguard peace. The state can - and must, if necessary - eliminate force by stronger force. However, in doing so, it employs the very same means which actually endanger peace. And it can actually only ever employ these means in order to prevent more serious forms of force. The church's responsibility towards the state therefore, consists above all in reminding it and the whole society of the fact that a state of affairs (be it internal or external), which is kept stable by force alone, does not mean peace but involves rather the utmost threat to peace.

e) However, it cannot be denied that the absence of war is indeed an aspect of peace. And the decisive question is, therefore, whether the absence of war may be guaranteed in any other way than by the threat and - *ultima ratione* - by the use of military force. Today, it is popular to engage in arguments which make allusion to the fact that it was just the military balance between both military blocs which had the effect of preventing war in Europe, and that the renunciation of the threat of military force would thereby be a renunciation which would threaten peace. In whatever way this argument is to be assessed, one thing must be clear: a decision is only politically responsible if it considers the consequences, side effects, and risks of this decision. This also has to be considered with regard to the theological demands on the legislator. A demand which tended to excuse the state from responsibility for the consequences, side-effects, and risks possibly connected with this decision, would be theologically and morally reprehensible. It would contradict the fundamental intention of Barmen V, in terms of which the state has to act "according to the yardstick of human insight and human capability".

f) Can the church, in spite of this, insist that every use of military force is against God's will and therefore that even the *threat of military force*, institutionalised in the form of armies, is also to be condemned absolutely?[64]

---

[64] For it is irrefutable that the threat of force is only appropriate if its use follows when worse comes to worst, and that the state which threatens with force must be prepared to use it. It would simply be irresponsible to raise the enormous financial, physical, and psychologi-

The church can probably only do this in the sense that it demands that the states express this condemnation themselves. Only by describing every war as an offence against God's gracious and - precisely, in its graciousness - holy will, can the church formulate the urgent demand on all states worldwide to condemn solemnly and together the mere threat of military force. Is this really something unreasonable, according to the standard of *human insight* ? Is it not, rather, *imperative* according to the standard of human insight?

If I am not altogether mistaken, it will be possible to bring about general agreement within Christianity concerning the condemnation of war, as a means by which the state might fulfil its task of providing for peace. Evangelical synods and church leadership, catholic bishops and bishops' conferences, and (since Pius XII) even popes have sent similar signals, with greater or lesser firmness. But there has been a continual lack of boldness and personal courage. Unfortunately, Pius XII, at the time of the so-called Cold War, did not remain faithful to his opinion proclaimed at the end of 1944, that every theory of a military solution

cal investments which are necessary at present for the threat of military force if one was not prepared to use this force in the case of an emergency.

to conflict had become obsolete. The Evangelical Church in Germany has not withdrawn the clear theological insight that, in accordance with God's will, there ought to be no war. However, this has certainly not been extended to include the statement that, in accordance with the will of God, there is also no place for the institutionalised threat of military force. Following through the course of theological thought from the principal rejection of war to the rejection of the institutionalised threat of military force, one has come across an *obstacle* which up to this point has proved to be insuperable.

Is it of a theological nature? Is it theologically grounded? If it also belongs to the foundations of theological ethics to consider and to take into account the possible consequences of a decision (in this case, the possible political consequences of a theological decision) then one is obliged to answer this question in the affirmative. For clearly it is uncertainty with regard to the consequences of a condemnation of the institutionalised threat of military force which allows this obstacle to emerge. If the theological condemnation is taken seriously at the political level on only one of the opposing sides and if, therefore, the institutionalised threat of military force is unilaterally withdrawn, then the very thing which is to be prevented could be provoked: war. Consequently, we are left with this obstacle which is given expression in the approval of competing military powers and which lives from the bold hope (*a posse ad esse non valet consequentia*) that the step from potentiality to reality is best hindered precisely through this potentiality.

One must take this obstacle seriously. Obscuring it by rhetoric only threatens to increase anxiety. This obstacle will hardly be overcome by invoking the possibility of those apocalyptic consequences which could result from the perpetuation and further development of military potential. For we just do not know which of the possible results of our decisions will become reality. If one could, with a leap back from the present state of competing military potentialities, return to a political *status quo ante* on the arms question, then it would probably be relatively easy for agreement to be reached, even among the politicians of the factions which so distrust each other. But it is just this leap backwards which is impossible. Military know-how will not be forgotten in the memory of humankind. And, in the same way, an analogous jump forward seems equally impossible. It only takes an awkward fact - such as the fact that Iran is carrying out a religiously motivated war at the moment - for the obstacle to be reinforced.

Nevertheless, if we are supposed to be able to overcome this, then the impossible leap will require to be replaced by a long series of steps. This will, without doubt, have to involve a well-defined and limited renunciation of sovereignty as a *finis intermedius*. This (by analogy with the threat and use of force by the police in internal politics) is permissible in the context of the collective responsibility of all states, in order to prevent the solution of international conflicts with the aid of national military force (or its escalation by corresponding alliances). This has nothing whatsoever to do with the utopian view of a political order which makes no recourse to the legitimate use of force. In no way can a demand addressed to the legislator and which is grounded in the Gospel be so naïve. For the Gospel is rather the word to the sinner of the forgiveness of sins. Nothing in the world reckons more seriously with the reality of evil than the Gospel. However, it does not follow from that that we should demand a state that is as heavily militarised as possible. It concerns much more the urgent request for the *limitation* of the legitimate use of force within the political order as it is represented by the institution of the state. The failure to date of the kind of projects of which the United Nations stands as a sad example is due not least to the fear which the national states have of a limited and well-defined renunciation of sovereignty. Because of this, providing for peace today requires the urgent setting aside of this fear.

This will require many cautiously considered steps. But the church would now have to take part in this *as a pace-setter*, by overcoming that obstacle with this process in view and by making it perfectly clear that it is theologically mandatory to remove the institutionalised threat of military force (which is institutionalised in the form of rival military powers). This should certainly be done step by step, but not by creeping around on tip-toe or by marching on the spot - rather, by placing one foot in front of the other such that we really do stride forward and make progress. The institution of war can only be abolished if the institution of the potential for war is abolished. Increasingly, day by day, the paradox formulated in Rom 7:19 - the good that I would, I do not, but the evil I would not, I do - casts its shadow over our intention to avoid war by means of the threat of military force.

The insight (that it requires a whole series of steps in order to make progress on the way to removing rival military potentialities) should by no means hinder the church from taking the first step which it certainly can take in this respect. It ought to overcome this straightforward obstacle and, functioning *as a pace-setter* in and through these political steps, condemn every institutionalised threat of military force, along with all war, as action directed against the will of God. Whether as conscientious objectors or as soldiers, this would mean for Christians that (while clearly not having to carry out anything as absurd as 'the subversive demoralising of the troops') they would have the responsibility for generating an awareness of the paradoxical nature of our military existence. Better still, it would mean that they would have a duty to raise further the awareness of all the responsible military personnel and politicians who are already conscious of this paradox. Thereby, they would assist in its abolition. To those Christians doing military service there falls, in this matter, a particularly weighty task. To seek to deny, in a fit of spiritual - or rather, carnal - arrogance, the seriousness with which human beings are Christians, and are continually trying anew to be Christians, should be totally unacceptable.

Generating and raising the awareness of the paradoxical nature of our human existence (for the purpose of removing the paradox) will only reach its goal, however, if there is also a corresponding raising of consciousness in those who may oppose this. Following this line, the church would have to prepare an urgent demand calling upon those states which still operate with the threat of force as a means of the prevention of war to name the clearest preconditions for their application. These states would have to make it clear in a convincing way that the means of military force is understood by them only as a provisional arrangement, which must itself be withdrawn as quickly as possible, because the goal intended with these means - peace - is itself (at the very least) the opposite of the use of military force. They will have to admit and take into account the fact that the means of military force endanger the goal which they are supposed to serve and therefore must be modified for the sake of the goal so that they *can* no longer come to be used. Accordingly, the church will have to bring the state to the point where it develops alternative concepts of security and sees to the fact that the means of military force *can* only ever be used for defensive purposes for as long as agreement has not been reached about their abolition.

g) In this sense the church today has to ask in a totally new way the old question whether the state of being a soldier stands to be blessed by God, and probably has to answer it completely differently from the way Luther did. This question requires to be asked anew, inasmuch as it can no longer be asked in an individualistic way whether I forfeit eternal salvation by not objecting to military service. Rather, it is important to ask whether *the church* can credibly proclaim the Gospel, the glorification of those who make peace, without at the same time rejecting *every* threat and use of military force. And how can it do this more convincingly than by working for the laying aside of weapons not only by Christians, but by all people around the world (*kath'holen ten oikoumenen*)? If the necessary steps toward this are not further to be put at risk by the nations, then the question forces itself inexorably on the church, whether the time has not come in which Christians can only be credible witnesses to Jesus Christ as conscientious objectors.

I have formulated *questions*. How I myself answer these questions should have become clear. However, it is not my answer but the answer of the church, as it expresses the consensus of believers, which is sought. Barmen itself was at first merely a question put by some teachers of the church to the Christian congregation.[65] The congregation at that time gave the answer in the form of a synod, which to-

---

[65] Karl Barth laid great stress on the fact that his formulations could first of all only be a *question*, which only the congregation can *answer* while identifying itself with this question. He had already expressed it in this way at the Free Reformed Synod of Barmen-Gemarke. Cf. J. Beckmann, loc. cit., 34.

day is characterised as embodying both spiritual and worldly courage. To encourage such bravery, not before the enemy but before ourselves, is no longer the role of the theologian. It is the work of the Holy Spirit who speaks to us through the one Word of God, whom on this matter we are to hear and also to trust and obey, both in life and in death.

It may be that today this one Word of God proves, above all, to be the stumbling block of our political existence. This in fact it is, both from a worldly and a spiritual point of view. To those to the left it is foolishness, to those to the right it is scandal. But if the political existence of Christians bears witness to Jesus Christ as the Word of God who is fundamentally confusing to (indeed, who reduces to absurdity) the apparent plausibilities of those to the left and to the right, then what is witnessed is theological existence in the sense of the Barmen Declaration. In this case, we would have understood that the Synod of the 31st of May, 1934, wishes neither to be celebrated in retrospect nor inherited, but desires, rather, to continue on in our own decision-making. We would then have appreciated the essence of Barmen as expressed in the judgement of Karl Barth: "a call forwards".[66]

[66] K. Barth, in : *Texte zur Barmer Theologischen Erklärung*, loc. cit., 172.